Ageing and Change in Pit Villages of North East England

Ageing and Change
in Pit Villages of
North East England

By Andrew Dawson

ISBN: 9781921775307

Published by
University of Melbourne
Custom Book Centre

December 2010

All rights reserved. No part of this publication may be reproduced or transmitted in any form or by any means, electronic or mechanical without permission in writing from the Author.

Ageing and Change in Pit Villages of North East England

Andrew Dawson

Andrew Dawson is Professor of Anthropology at the University of Melbourne. He has researched and written extensively on the issues of post-industrialism and mobility. His books include *Migrants of Identity* (with N. Rapports, eds), *After Writing Culture* (with A. James and J. Hockey eds) and *The Impacts of International Migration* (with G. Craig, S. Hutton, N. Roberts and M. Wilkinson).

CONTENTS

Abbreviations

Preface

INTRODUCTION ...1

METHODS ...3

PART I-BACKGROUND

Introduction....19

1-The Ashington Area: Definition and Location ... 19

2-Historical Background ...20

3-People, Contexts, and Means of Contact ...64

58 Footnotes ... 73

PART II-COMMUNITY AND CHANGE

Introduction ...74

1-The Representation and Celebration of Community ...75

2-Change and the Reconstitution of an Idealized Community ...123

Footnotes ... 150

PART III-ISSUES OF THE AGEING PROCESS

Introduction ...153

1-Transition and Continuity in Old Age ...154

2-Social Relations Between the Elderly: Association and Conflict ...204

3-Responses to the Physiological Realities ...246

Footnotes ...274

CONCLUDING COMMENTS ...275

Glossary ... 282

Bibliography ...287

ABBREVIATIONS

A.C.	Age Concern.
A.C.C.	Ashington Coal Company.
A.M.F.	Ashington Miners Federation.
B.A.C.M.	British Association of Colliery Managers.
B.C.	British Coal.
Buffs	Royal Antediluvian Order of the Buffaloes club.
E.S.R.C.	Economic and Social Research Council.
I.L.P.	Independent Labour Party.
N.A.C.O.D.S.	National Association of Colliery Oversmen, Deputies and Shotfirers.
N.C.B.	National Coal Board.
N.U.M.	National Union of Mineworkers.
N.U.P.E.	National Association of Public Employees.
W.M.C.	Working Men's Club.
W.R.V.S.	Women's Royal Voluntary Service.

PREFACE

Britain's coal mining communities are often regarded as exemplars of the working class community without compare. However, to what extent can it be said that such communities persist in the face of the loss of their material referent. Britain's coal industry has been in dramatic decline since the 1950s, and that decline became almost terminal following the Miner's Strike of 1984-85. In this book I consider this question in relation the generation of elderly mining people of Ashington in Northumberland. Once the 'largest mining village in the world', coal mining is now all but finished in Ashington. What becomes clear is that the idea of a coal mining community persists as a resource that is central in the mediation of life's crises. The book is a slightly modified version of an unpublished doctoral thesis completed in 1990 at the University of Essex. Notably, its social historical statement developed through Part I has been dramatically paired back following the publication of Kirkup and Thompson's excellent, *The Biggest Mining Village in the World* (1993), a more detailed analysis than my own. In its place I provide mere necessary background for the reader and an exposition of some of the key and original arguments presented in the original thesis, in particular, its deconstruction of a commonplace depiction of the Ashington Coal Company as a benevolent capitalist enterprise. The book is based on research carried out in the late 1980s and is, then, a valuable snapshot of community in the immediate strike era. The scholarly attention given to mining communities during the strike was not replicated in the years that followed. As such, this is one of the few anthropological accounts of its type, of post-industrial England (see Charlesworth, 1993) and of ageing in that context in particular (see Degnen, forthcoming). Much of my research career subsequently has been devoted to considering post-industrial life in England in a longer timeframe, and publications of this ilk draw partly on material presented in this book, particularly articles and book chapters on mining and mobility (1998), gender (2000) and the ageing body (2002) that share data and argumentation with Parts I/II, III.1 and III.3 respectively.

I owe a debt of thanks to several people, without whom the book would not have been possible. I thank the people of Ashington and, particularly people at the Woodhorn Colliery Museum for badgering me to make the contents of my thesis more easily available. I am flattered. The book is a product of the very earliest phase of my research career, and I only hope that its freshness and detail outweighs some of its naivety. What intellectual sophistication it exhibits is partly a product of the assistance of others. I thank Professor Judith Okely and the late Dr Ian Craib for their encouragement and the brilliance of their insights. I thank Professor Nigel Rapport and Professor Leonore Davidoff whose comments of examination and review were so insightful. Most importantly, I thank my parents, Mabel and

Wilfred Dawson, my best friend, Paul Clark, and, of course, my wife, Kotoyo Hirano-Dawson, for reasons too numerous to mention here.

INTRODUCTION
This ethnographic study looks at the socially constructed and historically and culturally specific ageing process and experiences of ageing amongst the elderly in the mixed aged setting of a group of mining communities in north east England. The fieldwork took place in the area of Ashington in Northumberland between March 1986 and September 1987, a key period of mine closure. Few ethnographic studies of the elderly have been done and none have been done in this particular area. Some studies have concentrated on day centres (Hazan, 1980)) or homes for the elderly (Hockey, 1987) and few have looked the aged as part of the wider community. The fieldwork for my study was carried out in a range of formal and informal contexts (day centres, clubs for the elderly, working men's clubs, parties, home visits, etc.). Moreover, whilst much of my work concerns institutions designed specifically for the use of the elderly, these provided a platform for research in other mixed age contexts. The study examines the experiences of the aged in their 'total' social context. Other studies have concentrated on beleaguered ethnic minorities; for example Hazan's (1980) study of a Jewish day centre in north London and Myerhoff's (1978) study of a home for elderly Jews in north America. In contrast, the formal contexts (particularly the clubs for the elderly) where much of my research was carried out are unique in relation to other leisure arenas in the area of study in that t1hey are often characterized by a widely differentiated

social mix (see also Jerrome, 1988). Others have been highly specific in the questions they confront; for example, Hockey's (1987) concern with the elderly's encounter with dying. This study concerns the 'whole life' of the elderly. A broad range of issues, determined primarily by their salience in fieldwork interactions, are considered in the context of ageing; as attitudes, responses and conditions reflecting this specific ageing process. My study also represents a movement away from the tendency in much gerontological literature to study the elderly as a problem; medical, welfare (Townsend.1965), as isolates (Tunstall.1966), demographic or otherwise. The manners in which the elderly positively respond to crises of ageing and resist control and denigration stemming, in part, from others' problematizing of their condition is highlighted. Oral historians have viewed and used the elderly as a source of information. I emphasize that in responding to problematic aspects of their lives, the elderly use their life histories similarly, i.e. as a resource. After the following section on methodology the book is divided into three parts. The first provides essential information about the geographical location of the area, its history since the inception of the mining industry, and the contexts in which my research was carried out. The second concerns representations by the elderly of community and change. The third deals with a series of interrelated issues of the ageing process; culturally constructed notions of the transitions which take place in the ageing process, differentiation, conflict and association between the elderly, and, finally, perceptions and responses of the elderly to physiological ageing. Throughout I represent the ageing process as subject to change in the context of an area which since the inception of the mining industry has been governed by turbulence. I also emphasize the centrality of mining. Mining lies behind the growth and structural development of the area, and the majority of Ashington's residents have, either directly or indirectly, been dependent on it. Mining is central to the past of the contemporary aged. It underpins their notions of community and features of their social environment. And, changes within the industry itself have had a profound effect on the ageing process.

METHODS - ME, THEM AND US

At this point I will concentrate on a series of issues relating to the process of research. First, I will briefly describe the techniques and strategies of research used and the process of analysis. I suggest that pressures, exerted primarily by the research sponsoring body, led to compromises in the planned research strategy which were, ultimately, counter-productive, Secondly, I will turn to the questions of key elements of my life history, the specificity of our (myself and the elderly participants) respective identities, how we perceived one another, how we used one another, and other aspects of the nature of our relationship. With these questions in mind the behaviour in the contexts I worked in, the data produced and selected for integration in the text, and specific problems encountered in fieldwork are examined. To talk of the specificity of identity is to talk of an issue of manifold complexity; incorporating, for example, an awareness of gender, ethnicity, historico-social categories (Okely, 1989), etc. My intention here is to concentrate on the questions of age (young researcher/participant-elderly participant) and my relationship to the context as someone from nearby and with long standing family connections.

The Process of Research

The methodological stance adopted is that of ethnography, using participant observation, informal interviews, and local 'cultural' documents. Selection of concepts is largely determined by their applicability to the substantive issues of importance which become apparent in the processes of fieldwork and data analysis. I started from participant observation then, having developed a series of contacts, this was supplemented by non-directive interviews. As substantive issues of importance became more apparent, this was supplemented by more directive interviews. As more confidence grew between myself and the people I worked with, a series of more adventurous techniques, strategies and sources of data were used; group interviews, the audio recording of interaction in the leisure arenas of the elderly people I worked with, use of the videos they made of their parties and other social events, and reporting back of interpretive developments in the form of small seminars organized and suggested by club participants (see below). The direct quotes which appear in the text are from field notes made during participant observation or transcribed interviews and group conversations. It was also my intention to enter the field with few foreshadowed research problems. This was justified by a belief in the elderly themselves illuminating the issues of importance within their lives, a belief in the efficacy of a serendipitous approach to research, and a fear of confirming stereotypes. It seemed to me that the pre-fieldwork identification of an elaborate body of problems would run the risk of beginning research from the premise of treating ageing as merely problematic. Having said this, I cannot hide the tensions of reconciling the approach recommended by, on the one hand, my own ideas and the sound advice of my supervisor, and, on the other, the demands of the sponsoring body. I overcame the demand for the specification of, 'the hypothesis being tested' (E.S.R.C.1987) by ignoring it, but, under pressure from peers going the 'right way about research' and the advice of the sponsoring body, I aborted my initial plan to enter the field immediately. I had been warned,

"*Research students are sometimes tempted to begin work*

on data collection and primary materials before they have completed the reading of articles, books and theses bearing upon their subject. It is essential, however, to acquire a thorough knowledge of what work has been done in a field before a new contribution can be adequately planned. This involves the construction of an adequate bibliography; a careful combing of registers of abstracts and other guides to research in progress; a systematic review of the professional journals; and a careful reading of the relevant books and monographs." (E.S.R.C.,1984:7).

After discovering that nobody else had completed a project of the kind I intended to work on, I went on to compile an extensive literature review which was based, partially on issues I had worked upon in previous research on the elderly, and which reflected my planned serendipitous approach to the new research, i.e. it was suitably eclectic. The project was great fun and I learnt a lot, but it was less than fruitful beyond that I had completed another E.S.R.C. first step specification; details of the literature review are required for presentation in their continuation forms. On going into the field, I returned to my initial plan.

Ashington and Me: A Stranger at Home

The brief for my research, ageing in mining communities of North East England, was specified by the E.S.R.C. linked studentship and was in conjunction with my supervisor's research (see Okely.1988). My aptness for the post stemmed from the interest I had developed in the issue of ageing in previous research work, and my connections with the North East and mining communities particularly (see below). Nevertheless, Ashington was the last place I thought of going to. It was too close to home. I valued my private life and had developed too many naughty habits I didn't want Mam and Dad to see. Privacy would be impossible in an area where both sides of the family come from. Moreover, though my mother and father had moved out of Ashington to nearby Morpeth (almost the only ones) my mother still worked there. In my heart I dreamed of working in the mining communities of sunnier climates; Asturias perhaps. At the time of going about finding a place where to work, these same hedonistic motives played the most important part in selection. A desire to reaffirm acquaintances with my beloved Sunderland football club took me initially to county Durham, and then, after being unable to find accommodation in the mining villages there, I turned to a part of Northumberland where I was politely warned off the stomping ground of other social scientists I contacted, and whom I shall not name. To my expectant parents (who were waiting for the return of the errant son) I had justified my desire not to go to Ashington with spurious social scientific rhetoric. My mother was unable to question this, but she saw straight through it, and carefully engineered my temporary residence in the town; "come to meet me from work darling and Aa'll introduce you to a canny man who can tell you aall aboot the pit." It seemed like a good idea. This nice man got me drunk, and suddenly Ashington seemed like a place abundant with research possibilities. Just by chance he also knew of a very cheap flat that was going. The next day I was living in Ashington.

Of course, there is no such thing as 'just' a visiting ethnographer, but my family connections rendered this part of my identity of largely forgettable significance to the people I worked with. Almost everybody knows or knows of my relations. Both sides of the family are large, spread throughout almost all of the constituent areas of Ashington and, with the exception of my parents and one aunt and uncle, my parents' generation are all mining people who had representatives in many of the local pits. Additionally, my mother's family are accorded a degree of fame by the fact that her brother, Ronnie Turnbull, was a local sporting hero. I was often located in a known family history and seen as an Ashingtonian. I wasn't visiting; for most of the people I worked with I had come home to, or, as far as they knew, had never left. In fact, I had never lived there. My position was essentially contradictory. I was a stranger in what many seemed to regard as my home. Perhaps the prime exemplification of this contradiction concerns language. Given the local and occupational specificity of the Pitmatic (a term used to describe local language because its vocabulary draws extensively on mining, I had, paradoxically, for someone who grew-up just down the road, considerable problems of language, which made, again paradoxically for a male ethnographer, research amongst women often much easier than with men among.

There were, of course, considerable advantages in the position I faced. Most importantly, some of my relatives proved to be excellent informants (throughout and after fieldwork) and contacts, introducing me to other informants and easing me into social contexts, particularly the working men's clubs, which would otherwise have been more difficult. Moreover, there was also congruence between data supplied by the people I worked with and family history, some of which I have an intimate knowledge of. I am convinced that the victim in the story supplied by club participants to warn of the dangers of marriage in old age was my maternal grandfather. However, the family connections proved double edged. My mother's engineering of my residence in Ashington was the first sign of my movement back into a sphere of family influence and control which I, having left home at a relatively early age, had never really learnt how to deal with. This was to prove ethically problematic. My presence quite literally scared a group of people from attending the contexts I entered. Ethnographers are warned of the political aims of the sponsoring bodies and the use to which their data may be put (see, for example, Okely (1987)). In my case, I needed to be aware of my family in such respects. Members of my mother's family were present in two of the clubs for the elderly I worked in. After some weeks of beginning fieldwork, my mother's sister-in-law, my aunt Olive, unexpectedly left the club, and then, a few weeks later, was joined by others in her circle that followed her elsewhere. Her and my mother's unsolicited insistence that her departure had nothing to do with my presence led me to suspect the contrary. In retrospect I am convinced that her departure was related to my passing of information to her (about for example, pregnancies in the family, new jobs of family members) from my mother's brother Joe and his wife Charlotte who attended another club, and her accurate suspicion that my familial inquisitiveness about her life was, in part, prompted by the queries of the latter. I had never known Joe and Charlotte very well. They were the sought of relatives one only ever sees at weddings and funerals. I had always put this lack of contact down to the size of my mother's family. I was, however, to discover that the family was in fact fraught with tensions, and, moreover, that Joe had committed some great misdemeanour. These facts had been concealed in a family conspiracy of silence, and even now I know little other than what is stated. In retrospect it seems that I became an unwitting researcher/informant for one part of the family, Joe and Charlotte, whom, because of this mysterious misdemeanour, had been virtual outcasts in the eyes of Olive and my mother. My aunt Olive's departure from the club was, for her, necessary. Whilst she did not want me to be compromised and burdened with the conflicts of another generation of the family, and did not want to discourage the normal interest family members show in one another, her breaking of regular contact with me by departure from the club was a gesture to Joe and Charlotte that they had not been forgiven; that if their interest in the family shown by the passing of information to, and questioning of me was an attempt at familial reintegration it would not be tolerated. It was a gesture of the continuation of their social death within the family.

The Age Dimension

My sensibilities and preconceptions about the elderly (those of a young man) undoubtedly played a crucial part, albeit at an unconscious level, in the selection of relevant data. I cannot discount the possibility that the prominence I have given to sexuality and conflict above other issues may have resulted from the shock I felt at having embedded stereotypical notions I had held about the elderly in these respects so dramatically overturned by the antagonism and obscenity in much of the behaviour I encountered.

At another level it was clear that my presence as the sole young participant in many of the contexts played a part in relation to their momentary awareness of negative aspects of their social identity. A number of people acted uneasily in my presence, careful, for example, to criticize concert party acts that they would, perhaps, normally have enjoyed, joined in with (audience participation was encouraged), or appreciated as totemic symbols of 'good ageing'. I sensed that I had disrupted the normal ambience of club life by heightening the awareness of participants' conformity to stereotypical images of the elderly (such as, their constant enjoyment of dated nostalgic entertainment). This unease must also be understood in terms of my representing the threat of the potential invocation of negative stereotypes about the elderly which the likes of my age group are perceived to hold. However, in as much as I created a degree of unease, I was also a resource. Later in the book I show how I was actively utilized in the imaginative construction of a family group which served at one level to deflect the potential negative gaze of the younger other, and at another level served in the distancing of the women involved from the other elderly within the social context.

In the context of the Buffs my presence served another purpose. The club, or lodge, I attended faced the prospect of, quite literally, dying out. Its existence was becoming hard to justify to the higher authorities in the 'Buffaloes Order'. This threat became critical with the sudden death of the lodge leader, who had been central to a fight against the lodge's closure. His death prompted the immediate election of a new leader and a reshuffle of lower grade posts. This was a break with traditional Buffs practice which normally involves the delaying of appointments until after the funeral. Quite unexpectedly,

I, who had only been a member of the lodge for two months, was given a dramatic promotion to the grade of 'lodge constable'. The choice of post was far from arbitrary. One of duties of the lodge constable is to lead funeral processions, read the sermon, and lay a wreath on behalf of the other members. It was clear that I was used as a sign of resistance to the threat of closure; to represent, in the presence of representatives of the higher echelons of the order, the lodge's continuity.

Finally, I note later how I was used as a passive male catalyst of obscenity in the context of a women's birthday party. Similarly, in the absence of the type of role (drivers, table setters, etc.) which other young club participants (though there were few of these) in the clubs for the elderly held, it was as a catalyst to the usual jovial ambience that my primary role lay. Moreover, again my sexual identity was central in this respect. They began the process by teasingly pointing to any arbitrary evidence of my virility. For example, if I was seen in the high street bank talking to a young female cashier, as soon as club night came around people would tease me about having an affair with her. Through their encouragement I found myself forced into playing the comic role of the young male stud. Perhaps inevitably as young and old it was the different and polarized aspects of our identities, most notably, sexual young man and unsexual or, at least, sexually ineligible elderly, which became the key terrain around which much of our interaction was based. Men engaged in the teasing, offered me sexual advice, suggested potential partners and so on. Women derived fun out of the absurdity of a potential relationship with me. Christmas cards were sent to 'my man Andy', and received from, 'Hilda, your best girlfriend' and 'Evelyn your secret lover'; whenever we left the kitchen together, Mrs. Howie (the leader of a club I attended) put on a fake pant and adjusted her bra strap. Sometimes, however, the play got a little close for comfort as I became the victim of a quick grope by women daring the taboo in front of friends. Whitehead (1976) has commented on the licence given to a sexual content in ribald play between elderly men and young women. In my case the gender-age relationship was reversed.

This aspect of the nature of interaction between me and some of the elderly women proved to be a means by which I extended the scope of my fieldwork. Hilda, the comedienne, and I became close precisely because we had convergent interests. I was eager to establish a female informant and contact who could introduce me to the type of female networks, beyond the clubs, which were so difficult to participate in because of their informality. Hilda, on the other hand, saw me partially as the perfect aid to her image of comic deviant sexuality which she was compliant in cultivating. I was a mock toy boy to be showed off to her friends at coffee mornings, parties and so on.

Personal life history and the co-authorship of data

An implication of the above is that through playing these humorous and entertaining roles with one another we were involved in producing together what eventually became the data for the book. The data concerning community represents one step beyond this; we were co-authors in its production. One method used in the reporting back of data was the organization of small discussion groups and seminars based around broad themes such as 'the past and the present' and 'the history of Ashington'. In retrospect my reports contained little elucidation of the types of exaggerations and contradictions which were evident in their accounts of life histories, perceptions of community and of change, which I outline later. I reported back data I had recorded, edited, uncritically interpreted, and, effectively, embellished with literary sources.

At one level the discussions and seminars were a source of alternative entertainment to the often endless games of bingo, and my failure to elucidate these exaggerations and contradictions is in part explained by my fulfilling a dictum of performance, i.e. always please the punters. However, the fact that I only became fully aware of these exaggerations and contradictions in the process of analysing data in the post-fieldwork phase suggests more than this. Though idealized notions of community celebrated in the clubs do not serve the kind of roles in my life which they did for the elderly participants, such idealized notions are, nevertheless, central to my life history. The dualistic feelings my parents held about Ashington and life there (a grubby place they were glad to escape from, alongside recognition that the qualities they admire in themselves have their roots in specific features of life in Ashington) are in part mirrored in my own feelings about the place and its people. Additionally, the negative feelings I held towards the place as a child were transformed through subsequent years, particularly by my inhabitation of a liberal-left academic milieu. Though not a paradise, it and its people had become something I admired. The moment which euphorically crystallized this admiration came when I was in the field. On the night when most of Britain was ensuring the third return of the Thatcher government, the Wansbeck constituency almost doubled its Labour majority. What I want to emphasize is that I was, throughout the course of my fieldwork, in a state of euphoric admiration with regard to Ashington and its people. This admiration lay behind my own compliance in the uncritical celebration of the type of idealized notion of community practiced in the clubs. My compliance lay, primarily, in this act of reporting back, where I, effectively acted as a crucial stimulant to this celebration.

The Future

James points out that one of the consequences of the rise of reflexivity in anthropology is that, "it forces us to come to terms with the incompleteness of our final interpretations."(1989:3). Throughout the period of writing up my book I have been reminded how seemingly arbitrary events may not only spark new interpretive insights, but that these new insights may indeed prompt a need for fundamental reinterpretation. For example, a recent illness which provoked a bout of mortality paranoia reminded me how an awareness of the relative imminence of their death was obviously crucial to understanding the elderly. This theme, which had formed the central tenet of my undergraduate thesis on ageing had been bypassed in a sub-conscious rejection of all that I had done before, in the quest for personal development. Research on the question of ageing, and most particularly, the realization that my experience of inhabiting a relatively early stage in the life cycle is critical in selection of data and interpretation, and, serves to heighten awareness of the importance of the kind of 'dialogical' approach to ethnography where one looks at both personal changes and historical changes in the society in question over a number of years (Caplan, 1988:10). In my case this will not be done merely as a means of improving the quality and honesty of my ethnographic work. Moreover, life chances which may deprive me of the potential of continuing doing full-time ethnographic work cannot halt this endeavour. My intimate attachment to the area and people of my research make this an endeavour from which, happily, I cannot escape.

PART I
BACKGROUND

This part of the book provides a body of essential background information. It is divided into three sections. The first concerns location, the second provides historical information, and the third gives details of the contexts in which I worked. It serves to contextualize the book, particularly in that I attempt to outline critical life history experiences of the elderly people I worked with, and historical changes in the experiences of ageing, the constitution of the elderly as a social category, and the relationship between the elderly and younger generations.

1-THE ASHINGTON AREA: DEFINITION AND LOCATION

According to official geography the term Ashington refers only to the town of that name, but it is commonly understood to refer to the town and a series of its satellite villages; Lynemouth, Ellington, Linton, and, more debatably, Guide Post, Stakeford, Newbiggin-By-The-Sea, and Pegswood. The common identity stems from the centrality of Ashington town as an urban and commercial centre, the previous dominance in the area of the Ashington Coal Company, and their commonality as mining communities (1).

Ashington is situated in the southern part of mid-east Northumberland approximately twenty miles north of Newcastle-Upon-Tyne in the heart of what was the Northumbrian coalfield. It is bordered to the north by countryside and rural farming, fishing, and mining communities. To the north-west and west it is bordered by predominantly a rural area, and to the south-west it is bordered by rural area and the market town of Morpeth. To its south are the towns of Bedlington, Blyth, and Cramlington New Town, and their satellite villages. Like Ashington, the towns to the south, with the exception of Cramlington, which has grown in recent years through light industry, owe their development to the mining industry.

2-HISTORICAL BACKGROUND

Charlie Burnsey 96 year old ex-miner, ex-faith healer and, 'Ellington's unpaid preacher on the meaning of life':

"It's a funny thing bein' owld. Sometimes it seems like greet holes appears in ya mind. It's enough t' get some folks doon wi' worry. But aall tell ya man, unless ya unlucky, the last thing that gans is ya mind. Ya knaa when ya ask a bairn wat ees been doin' wi eesell......ee giz ya a greet lang explanation from start t' finish wi' ney bits cut oot. Owld folks..we're aall alike....owld folks is the other extreme. Ya gan on editin' aall ya life an' ya nivver stop. Ya keep aall the

important moments. Nee matter how small ....even porsonal fragments. Theyor still important. An' as quick as aall them bits gans missin' the' can come back an' gan together in some varrie funny ways. Somebody'll remind ya an' the' back like the' clear as crystal."

My concern in this section of the book is to present an account of Ashington's history which makes central these 'important moments' or significant events, and the significant constant features of life in the area that the people I worked with pointed to in characterizing their life historical experiences. They were selected entirely, though not as part of any conscious endeavour, by the elderly people I worked with. The starting point in the construction of my account and research in this respect was usually such 'personal fragments'; personal images which frequently symbolize wider events. Nevertheless, I also draw on historical records, and conversations and interviews with local historians, local politicians, and union and colliery officials. I particular, while I disagree with many of its interpretations, I draw considerably on Gordon's *The Economic and Social Development of Ashington* (1959). Until the release of Kirkup and Thompson's *The Biggest Mining Village in the World'* (1993), it was a standard source for historical knowledge on the area, and it remains a remarkably valuable piece of scholarship. Whilst not wanting to lose sight of the experiences and perceptions of history of the people I worked with, my overwhelming concern is to develop a wider account of the macro-social, economic, and political processes behind the historical priorities they pointed to. My account is divided into three sub-sections. Whilst drawing on oral historical material, the first concentrates on these macro-social, economic and political processes. I will discuss a number of issues; growth of the urban area and population, infrastructural problems and development, strike history, employment make-up, social differentiation, social mobility, etc. Throughout I will emphasize the centrality of the mining industry and the policies of the coal company which formerly owned most of the pits in this area. Secondly, I will attempt to show how these macro phenomena were experienced by the people I worked with. I will discuss the nature of their financial existence, the working conditions faced by most, the implicit dangers in their lives, and the potential available to escape their existence. The unifying term used by the people I worked with to describe their experiences is hardship. As such, I will characterize their lives as a history of hardship, and will point to a series of images or personal fragments which are drawn upon by the elderly to symbolize this. Thirdly, I will discuss a number of significant changes and the extent to which in other respects elements of the past identified by the people I worked with have remained largely unchanged. At this point I will provide an impressionistic image of the area in the present day. A number of points should be made by way of justification of my account. Williamson states,

"The history of mining communities has been distorted by an almost exclusive emphasis on pit work, although pit work in the form we know it in the nineteenth and early twentieth centuries was only possible because of the way in which women worked in the home." (1982:118)

The implicit critique that most accounts of mining communities have been generic male histories can also be added to by pointing out that there has also been a tendency to focus on the mining population of these areas to the exclusion of other occupational groups. I accept entirely both points. However, writers such as Williamson himself and Szurek (1985) have more than adequately redressed the balance. In that I place mining and the coal company at the centre of my account I might be seen to be falling into the trap that is warned against. It is not enough to justify this emphasis by the facts that most of the people I worked with were mining people and mining people constitute the majority of Ashington inhabitants, and, secondly, that the history of mining in this area is in many respects unique in comparison to other areas and, as such, warrants detailed discussion. Rather, I justify my account at two other levels. As a male fieldworker I had, I feel, unique access to a specific type of information which I want to exploit. The second level of justification is to do with the centrality of mining in the lives of the people I worked with. I will show that for almost everyone in this area, men and women, mining and non-mining people, life and life chances were largely dependent on and controlled by the fluctuations of the mining industry and the social and physical structures of the area which were in themselves largely moulded by the mining industry and the coal company. Moreover, mining is, I would suggest, the central cultural referent by which life and the area are represented by the people I worked with. Given this, though I draw on information and arguments of writers such as Williamson and Szurek and the women I worked with, it is perhaps inevitable that I should concentrate on the information presented to me by my male/ex-miner informants, as they were the immediate agents of contact with the industry.

Finally, it should be emphasized that this type of account inevitably entails a preoccupation with specific moments to the exclusion of others, and an emphasis on specific aspects of life (most notably the characterization of life in Ashington as one of incessant hardship) throughout the epoch covered, to the exclusion of others. It is not enough merely to state that these are justifiable because these preoccupations reflect the concerns of the people I worked with. The aim of this part of the book is not merely to provide essential historical background. It will provide a platform from which the specific interpretations of history by the elderly, both of individuals and as they are constructed collectively in specific social contexts, play an important role within their lives. In other words I will, throughout the book, attempt to show why those moments are put back together in *'varrie funny ways.'*

MACRO SOCIAL, ECONOMIC AND POLITICAL PROCESSES

The Growth of the Mining Industry and the Consequent Growth of Population and Urban Area

Ashington town's status as an urban and commercial centre and, indeed, its very existence as a town are recent phenomena. Until the final years of the last century it too was a series of hamlets and villages. The official identification of the town's districts reflects the separate villages which, through their growth, merged and adopted a collective name from Ashington farm which was located in the old hamlet of Fell-Em-Doon.

The population growth which facilitated this process of urban merger, the growth of the satellite villages, and, indeed, the very inception of some of these villages was a direct result of the growth of the mining industry. Before the sinking of the first major pit in 1867 in what was to become Ashington town the mining industry consisted of a few small pits and scattered outcrop workings employing few men and women. However, the sinking of this pit was followed in rapid and steady succession by the sinking of a mass of others in the Ashington area. In the peak years of mining, from the turn of this century up to the nineteen fifties, there had been over two hundred collieries and other coal workings in the Northumberland coalfield. The Ashington area accounted for the greatest single concentration of these, and the highest levels of production within the region and among the highest in the country. Such unprecedented growth gave rise to Ashington town's description as, 'the biggest mining village in the world'. Up to 1850 from the turn of the century the total population of the settlements which now constitute Ashington town fluctuated between four hundred and fifty and five hundred and fifty. Over the following eighty years that figure was to increase by almost sixty times, immigrants flocked to take up work in the new deep mine developments. A peak of around thirty thousand was reached in the mid nineteen twenties, at the same time as the sinking of new pits and the expansion of the mining industry was tailing-off.

The Ashington Coal Company and the Urban Infrastructure

The explosive population growth gives rise to the characterization of Ashington in its early years as a 'pioneer community' (Gordon, 1954:40), or, more commonly, amongst the people of Ashington, as a 'gold rush town'. Like gold rush towns, in counterbalance to the potential of high earnings, Ashington suffered the problems of population growth in a hitherto underdeveloped area. However, the majot collieries owner, the Ashington Coal Company, played a central role in the filling of this vacuum. Notably, by 1934 it had built and owned 37% of the houses in the town of Ashington (N.U.M., Northumberland.1988).

This and the A.C.C's many other infrastructural investments gained for it a reputation as a model business enterprise and employer. However, the image of benevolence, a terms frequently used by Gordon (1959), for example, is contradicted at a number of levels. Amenities were of the lowest standards. It is also clear that the location and layout of urban development was planned around the exigencies of the industry, rather than with great respect to the quality of life. And, as one might expect, other elements of infrastructure were designed with profit maximization in mind, rather than the demands and preferences of ordinary Ashington inhabitants. For example, couching their objections in the language of the Quaker faith to which the coal owners subscribed, though above all fearing the consequences of alcohol consumption on production, the A.C.C. refused to allow the development of pubs on its land and prohibited the sale of alcohol from any of its property. The clearest indication of the misplaced positive identity of the A.C.C. is evident in the fact that the most substantial infrastructural improvements came not at the heights of the company's profitability, but, rather, in times of crisis when state intervention was necessitated. The most substantial improvements in housing came when the local council rebuilt to replace those houses devastated by air raids in the Second World War.

Improvements in sanitary facilities, and the beginnings of an integrated sewage system, came about in the depression years of the nineteen thirties, with government works grants for the unemployed.

Infrastructure, Company Policy and Control of the Workforce

What is above all else clear, I would argue, is that the very design of elements of the A.C.C. manufactured infrastructure served, and was largely planned to serve, alongside other company policy, in the direct and indirect control of the workforce. In particular, as I argue in copious detail in my doctoral this (1990), the development of a tied housing system, a piecework system and a lottery system – The Cavel – for allocating work and work in productive or less productive parts of the pit that was, nevertheless, underpinned by a minimum wage, were considerable draws for workers. This led, I argued to relative overpopulation in relation to available work in certain periods work.

I drew two main conclusion from this. First, the very objects of A.C.C. investment, most notably housing, which inform its image of benevolence, became the instruments by which the Ashington workers were directly controlled, through threat of eviction, for example. Secondly, they played a role in creating a reserve army of labour, which, it should be added, was periodically buttressed by workers from dwindling coalfields and agricultural areas to the south and north of the area, and which served to discipline the workforce. In explanation of the population influx which enabled this, and in further ramification of the image of benevolence, Gordon states, 'Recruitment was not difficult as Ashington, being a new undertaking, had no tradition of semi-feudal repression found in other mining districts.' (1954:26). What is clear is that where there was no tradition of semi-feudal repression such repression was soon recreated (particularly through the tied housing system, and other more subtle forms of ideological domination by the A.C.C., such as control of sections of the press.

Industrial Conflict

A number of writers have pointed to the 'traditional conservatism' of the Northumberland miners in comparison to their counterparts in other areas of the country (for example, Knowles (1952) and Newton (1969)). The studies which have produced these conclusions usually use strike propensity as the criterion of radicalism, and working hours lost through strike action as its main measure. Given that up until the late nineteen thirties the A.C.C. employees had had a relatively low incidence of industrial action, and given that the A.C.C. was by far the biggest mining enterprise in Northumberland, accounting for a large proportion of the total working hours in the coalfield as a whole, it is arguable that the Ashington miners were both the main cause of the conservative identity of the Northumbrian miners generally, and its prime exemplars. Indeed, the major thrust of Gordon's (1954) thesis is that the Ashington miners were characterized by a political restraint engendered by co-operative industrial relations, which, in themselves, were a consequence of the A.C.C's 'benevolent', post-feudal character. However, the conservative identity is, I would suggest, questionable, and fails to take into account the special circumstances faced by the Ashington miners which militated against the effectiveness of strike action. Trade union fragmentation, the endurance of the old craft unions, which were rarely predisposed towards radicalism, and a retarded process of trade union unification weakened the Ashington miner's political power which, as I have already established, was already undermined by the control directly afforded to the A.C.C. by its infrastructure, and by the constant threat of workers from both within and outside the area taking the jobs of the existent Ashington miners.

Given the circumstances it is perhaps a tribute to the people of the area that they were able on a few occasions to ensure the temporary closure of the A.C.C. collieries during bouts of industrial action. Most notable amongst these was the six month continuation of an all out strike preceding the ten day national general strike in 1926.

The clearest indication that the conservative identity is misplaced is evident in the industrial conflict during, and immediately preceding, the Second World War. The working population was significantly depleted by out-migration during the depression which had preceded these years, and national service conscription. Moreover, as the demand for coal rose sharply to fuel the war effort the pits were working at full capacity. The resultant near full employment and the years of experience of the A.C.C's repressive tactics heightened the political strength and solidarity of the miners, and their resolve to reverse their losses which had resulted from the cumulative wage suppression. The period was characterized by persistent and largely successful strike action whose frequency was generally greater than that in other coalfields. For example, in 1938 the A.C.C. collieries suffered more loss of time and output than any other coalfield in the U.K. (Gordon. 1954: 125).

Alternative Infrastructure

Inadequacies of the A.C.C. manufactured infrastructure were compensated for by the Ashington people's organization (largely under the auspices of bodies such as the Ashington Miner's Federation, the Co-operative Movement, and the Independent Labour Party) of alternative facilities. Most importantly, land was bought for the establishment of allotments, and the building of a series of working men's clubs and a co-operative store, which by the nineteen twenties had ten thousand members (McCullough-Thew, 1985). In a number of key respects the facilities were, however, more than merely compensatory.

The non-profit making feature of the organization of the co-operative store (McCullough-Thew, 1985) was extended in the case of the working men's clubs to that of positive redistribution. The clubs were affiliated to the Workers Federation Co-operative brewers which reimbursed profits to its affiliates. Instead of being paid back to the consumers of beer, the clubs used the reimbursements to provide for the retired, and for miner's widows, both of which groups were barely catered for by the A.C.C.

The facilities were also of significant value during industrial disputes. The allotments were crucial for the supply of produce throughout periods of strike action. Similarly, the co-operative store indirectly played a role in the continuation of strike action by offering low interest credit facilities.

In the case of the clubs, political considerations were a conscious feature of their design. For example, they were used to provide shelter for families evicted by the A.C.C., and as soup kitchens for the striking families. Some clubs also had a drinks levy which financed strike funds. This political element was evident from their inception. Committee members of organizations such as the A.M.F. and the I.L.P. were at first reluctant to sponsor the building of the clubs. Like the A.C.C. they feared the consequences of drunkenness. Their concern was not, however, for productivity or the religious sentiments of their Quaker employers. Rather, the fear was that it may legitimate a greater police presence which would ultimately give the A.C.C. a further source of control. However, the value of the clubs as centres for encouraging the politicization and solidarity of the Ashington men added to public pressure for their inception and prompted the decision for their construction to go ahead. Clubs performed the function of politicization in a number of ways . For example, as well as being meeting places, most hosted political events and established various political campaign committees. In conclusion I would suggest that in differing degrees such facilities were, for the ordinary people of the area, a real source of independence from, and power in relation to, the A.C.C., and represented a series of values, both implicit in the organization (non-profit, redistribution, etc.), and, in an articulated form (socialism), which were contrary to that which the A.C.C. represented (profit, competition and capitalism). In this sense such facilities represented not only an alternative/compensatory infrastructure, but also perhaps a counter structure.

Employment

Because Ashington's growth was due almost entirely to the growth of the mining industry it has, throughout its history, had a very narrow occupational mix. Until the industry began to be run down the vast majority of the wage earning population were miners or were employed in some other capacity (clerical officers, blacksmiths, engineers, etc.) by the coal companies and then, following nationalization in 1946, the National Coal Board. While the potential for men finding work outside the industry in the area was low, the job opportunities for women were almost non-existent. After women were barred from working in the pits they represented only a tiny minority of the wage earning population, occupying mostly clerical and retail service posts. However, a common theme amongst the people I worked with was that, at least until the development of on-site shower and laundry facilities at the pits, and the post-war renovation of housing facilities and revolution in the development of domestic labour saving devices, being a miner's wife was a full time job in itself. This point forms an integral strand within Szurek's (1985) book. She carefully argues that the domestic labour of the miner's wife is essential to the man's production.

The consequent dependence of miners' wives on the industry was shared generally even by most of the non-mining working population. Almost all work was either connected to the mines (i.e. in the supply industries or in industries which were dependent on coal) or was dependent on trade done with the mining people. In one way or another almost everyone was either directly or indirectly dependent on mining.

The potential to break the ties of this dependence by attempting to seek work outside of Ashington was also limited. Perhaps of greatest significance is the area's former isolation. Newcastle, the nearest major centre of non-mining employment, was a considerable journey, not feasible to undertake in a working day up until the Second world War when the transport system, which had been designed primarily to connect Ashington town with its satellite villages, many of which were cul-de-sacs, and the port of Blyth, was improved to take women to work in the munitions factories. Even when women's paid labour is deemed almost impossible, when necessary it is made possible. Secondly, the nature of mining work itself was a limiting factor in this respect. As most workers were unskilled labourers, or had learned trades specific to the industry, few had transferable skills.

Social Differentiation

In the absence of a strongly represented indigenous culture it is perhaps inevitable that coal mining has become the central cultural referent with which most people commonly identify or with which most people identify the area; it is the very reason for the development of the area, people's migration to it, and the resource on which most were dependent. Nevertheless, despite a low degree of occupational diversity, Ashington could never be described as socially homogeneous.

The diverse origins of Ashington's immigrants led the social historian Sid Chaplin to describe the area as a, "linguistic, social and intellectual boiling pot" (in Reed.1975:1). The earliest immigrants to the area were largely agricultural workers from Northumberland. Later immigrants, who continued to come to the area until the late nineteen twenties, were largely mining people from Northumberland, Durham, Cumberland, Cornwall, Scotland, Wales, and Ireland, and as far away as Poland and Italy. Despite the diversity of the origins of the early immigrants there was little ethnic identification, though the import of Irish sectarianism was widely reported.

Other differences, which, it should be said, Williamson has commented on extensively in his study of the mining village of Throckley (1982:66-72), include those concerning politics, intra-area localisms, and religion. However, perhaps the most significant social differences which appeared to have persisted in the context of my fieldwork experiences were of class, occupational status differentiation, differences based on perceptions of occupational group cultural characteristics, and differences based on day to day living at home and in the family sphere. I will return to class and occupational status differentiation (in the context of mining) in the following section on social mobility. Concerning differences based on perceptions of occupational group cultural characteristics, there is little bracketing off of occupational groups unless they are considered to be of a considerably high status. The fishing people of Newbiggin and the mining people, both of whom constitute residentially concentrated groups, are the only occupational sections of the working class singled out as possessing distinct characteristics. Both groups are often considered to be "superstitious". Most descriptions are polarized in attributing the mining people with complimentary (for example, 'kind', 'strong', etc.) or derogatory qualities. Mining people are often referred to as the prime cause of every negative characteristic of the area. People I spoke to characterized them variously as violent types, drinking people, and always financially frivolous. As one woman explained, "*Aall tell ya aboot the mining folk....Bingo, Bingo, Bingo.*"

Concerning differences based on day to day living, it is sufficient to say that classification is highly subjective, but that it is/was constructed upon perceptions of, for example, how people bring their children up, the financial order of their life, and domestic cleanliness. Despite the fact that they largely concern roles ascribed to women, they are, nevertheless, the concern of men and women alike. Williamson implies that they have a paradoxical significance, stemming from the degree of homogeneity of condition (or as he puts it, everyone being 'in the same boat') faced by ordinary mining people. He states,

"*Some families came to be labelled as particularly scruffy or unrespectable. They were not cut off socially but they represented a kind of benchmark against which the social status of the rest could be measured."* (1982:69).

Social Mobility

At this point I will discuss the limits to social mobility. Given the narrow degree of occupational diversity within the area, a consideration of the potential for occupational mobility in the context of the local mining industry must be central to the discussion. I outline two interrelated levels at which such limits can be identified: in the nature of the mining occupational structure and system of recruitment to mining management, and in deferential attitudes of the working class that serve to discourage promotion.

(i)Occupational structure and recruitment: An extended analysis of these was presented in the original thesis (Dawson, 1990) on which this book is based. I outlined eight basic categories of employee in the pit in broadly descending order of status and pay within official hierarchies from management, clerical staff, oversmen, deputies, skilled manual workers, hewers, overground workers and underground 'datal' workers. These grades and the hierarchy remained, I argued, roughly consistent from pre- to post-nationalisation of the industry. I demonstrated that the hierarchy was often instantiated beyond the pit in separate housing and so on. I demonstrated that mobility was difficult and that there were considerable class barriers to direct entry into

higher grades and promotion between grades. Nepotism was, I was often informed, a significant technique in this respect. However, I also argued, cultural barriers were generated by ordinary mining people that militated against their own occupational mobility. Central amongst these were derogatory labels – 'crawlers' (to management'), 'medlers' and 'unscrupulous men' - applied to oversmen and deputies, essentially liminal categories of staff between ordinary miners and management. These were significantly informed by contradictory aspects of their positions, as simultaneously, for example, guardians of safety and agents charged with maximising productivity. Currently, I am revisiting this classification, particularly with respect to how it was undermined by forms of alternative hierarchy. Notably, for example, 'stone men' who cut non-coal substances in clearing seams for ordinary miners to work are often treated with a respect that is not commensurate with salary. This, I have argued elsewhere (Dawson, 2002) is related to ideas about their ingestion of symbolically more polluting forms of dirt than coal, which is widely regarded as efficacious.
(ii)Deference: Edwardian Liberal MP, GFG Masterman famously stated that, *"There is not one high wall but two high walls between the classes and the masses and that erected.... by the exploited is the higher and more difficult to climb."* (1911:98). Hindrance to promotion in the pit and social mobility generally was not just a question of the

erection of barriers from above. Many ordinary mining people accepted their position within the class structure. At one level acceptance was a pragmatic response to the rigidity of the class structure. As one man explained to me,

"Aa knew Aa nivver wanted doon the pit, but Aa darsn't say it oot load. Me Motha and Fatha wanted better for us like. Wey Aa think that waz the same for aall parents. Ney Motha wants hor bairn gannin' doon that stinkin' dorty black hole, d' the'? But the' didn't want t' harbour silly dreams either. So Aa think that's why me Fatha used t' laugh when Aa telt wat plans Aa hed."

However, acceptance could also often be said to typify an ethos of deference. The same man went on to explain that, "Others waz see conservative man. Me aunt Mary used t' gi' me lugs a fair bashin'. "An' ee can rid yarsell o' them fancy ideas", shi used t' tell us...."An the trouble wi' ee is ya divvent knaa ya place". Wey wats ya place man? Aa thowt Aa hed as much right as anyone to get mesell a clean Job an' a better livin. Aa wazn't gannin doon ney bloody pit".

The proliferation of the type of deferential and 'conservative' attitudes outlined above is not at all surprising. They were stimulated, not only in the arena of work, but also within the very physical aspects of the ordinary mining people's living surroundings, from the name of the A.C.C. printed on public utilities, to the names of the houses in which they lived. Rows going by the names, not only of the coal owners, but also of established management families, stood alongside those named after national V.I.P's (members of the royal family, prime ministers, famous colonialists, etc.). In one section of rows houses were named, I was told, such that the first letter of the names of each row went together to spell 'ASHINGTON COAL COMPANY'. Other rows were named after local beauty spots or Shakespearian characters. In their design the rows were neither beautiful nor great works of art. Rows in one area, named simply, 1st, 2nd, 3rd, etc., and A, B, C, etc., more accurately reflected their uniform quality. The names symbolized, and acted as a constant reminder to the inhabitants of their insignificance, their inferior class origins and the power of management and the coal owners. The very ordinariness and familiarity of objects on which these physical reminders were placed must, I would argue, have added to the extent to which these relations of power and class took on a taken for granted appearance.

Despite the fact that I have argued a negative acceptance of the class system, there was also a sense in which it was subverted. However, rather than serving to challenge it in any concrete way, this positive act of subversion served in itself to strengthen the class system further. Again the manner in which the deputies were regarded is a useful illustration of this point.

The criteria which determined the low esteem of the deputies amongst ordinary miners went beyond those outlined earlier. One major source of criticism focussed on their perceived physical weakness and lack of stamina. They were considered unable to earn sufficiently in piece-work jobs. *"The dep'ty couldn't hew ees way active a paper bag'*, as the saying goes. Other men told me that many deputies entered the position because like many of the overground datal workers they were usually physically sick, a claim which is completely unfounded. Other criticisms of the deputy concerned a lack of intelligence. One popular local story tells of the man who, under pressure from his wife, reluctantly sits the exam for the deputies 'ticket' and returns home depressed, having found out that he has passed.

Wife: *"Wey how did ya get on?"*

Man : *"Aa passed."* Wife: *"Well done. Am very proud. An' wat did the' ask ya?"*

Man : *"The' asked us aall manner o' questions. Wats five times five, so Aa telt then twenty four. An' wats eight times eight, so Aa telt them sixty two."*

Wife: *"Had on a minute. Five fives is twenty five, and eight eights is sixty four!"*

Man : *"Aa knaa that. Am not stupid woman!"*

Wife: *"How did ya pass the exam then?"*

Man : *"The problem waz, Aa waz a damn bit closer than aall them that waz really tryin'."*

At one level such criticism was a mere elaboration of that which flowed in response to the deputy's invidious supervisory position. At another level such criticism was provoked precisely because the act of becoming a deputy was seen by many to represent a contravention of the ethos of deference to a managerial class (perceived as intellectually superior) or, alternatively, a lack of awareness and pragmatic adoption to the rigidity of the class system. The comments of one man I spoke to can be read both ways.

"There waz none mare stupid than the man that thowt ee hed it in him t' mek management, an he waz usually the deputy."

Whilst this is true, additionally, such criticism reflects a series of alternative status criteria which serve to subvert the official hierarchy where pay and supervisory status are paramount. Whilst deputies and oversmen were accorded the lowest position amongst workers in the pit, the stone men were, as I intimate above, the prime exemplars of these criteria. In general, values were placed upon actions which displayed qualities of little significance to the jobs of management. Mobility within the alternative hierarchy of ordinary miners not only corresponded to mobility within the official hierarchy. In so far as the jobs of deputy and oversman are of the lowest status, according to such criteria, movement into management was positively discouraged and resisted.

LIFE IN ASHINGTON: A HISTORY OF HARDSHIP

Most of the people I worked with described their early lives as being characterized by unrelenting hardship. The facets of this hardship were manifold.

An uncertain financial existence

For the mining people, the problems of surviving on what can be described, in comparison to current rates of earning, as generally meagre wages were compounded by constant income fluctuations. Such fluctuations were an incessant part of the day to day lives of the cavel workers. They came about because of the uncertainties of the cavel system itself, and the fact that the men worked with a natural, and thus wildly unpredictable substance. As one man explained to me,

"Ya didn't knaa where ya were. Ya could get wat ya thowt waz a good seam an' then hit stane, o' wettor an' afore ya knaa where ya are ya ruin' next t' nowt. It didn't matter how hard ya worked.... not if ya were hewin' shul loads o' pea soup. Mind, the next ya could be diggin' diamonds an' bye ya were happy."

The Cavel workers were not alone in facing such fluctuations. All were subject to changing wage agreements, and, to an extent, income changes brought about, ultimately, by the faltering progress of the seams through geographical barriers that affected the profitability of the pits. Many mining families, especially those not bound to the A.C.C. by occupancy of a company house, were prompted into speculative movement by the flow of news and rumours about changing agreements and potential and actual geological problems afflicting specific pits. This is undoubtedly one reason behind the comments of the former

Northumberland N.U.M. general secretary Sam Scott, whom Williamson cites. The Ashington miners were, *'just like gypsies, moving from one pit to the next even the chickens and geese used to lie on their backs every three months with their feet in the air ready to be tied up, put in a poke, and moved on to the next job.'* (in Williamson.1982:82).

Finally, it should be noted that incomes fluctuated with the ebbs and flows of the demand for coal. The A.C.C. cultivated only a minimal local market and was heavily reliant on exports, which were frequently hit in the volatile economic and political climate which has characterized Europe in the Twentieth Century; the century containing the largest portion of Ashington's total existence.

Given, as I pointed out earlier, the direct and indirect reliance of those not employed in mining on the prosperity of the mines and miners, such fluctuations were a reality for almost all inhabitants of the area. Life in Ashington as a whole, not merely for the miners, has been one of bondage to the uncertainties of both nature and a world far beyond its boundaries.

Work and working conditions

In addition to being physically strenuous, pit work entails considerable discomfort, fear, and danger. Whilst the conditions precipitous of these varied between pits (for example, the spacious seams and roadways of some pits, to the narrow seams of others, which often required men to work on their backs), conditions in the Ashington pits generally, though not particularly bad, were not particularly good either. All suffered problems common to pits in general, such as the heat and the dust. A series of other problems were common to Ashington pits in particular. All suffered from excessive water content. One man told me that it was not uncommon to spend a shift with most of the body immersed, such that, on walking home from the pit on a cold winter's day, steaming clothes quickly turned to ice. Secondly, I was told, the Ashington pits suffered from particularly high noise levels because of the slate content in the earth; as the earth slowly falls to settle on the roof beams it makes an incessant high pitched screeching noise.

The working conditions of the miner's wives were controlled by the pit and entirely at the mercy of all its uncertainties. For many women there was often little let-up in the work. They were called upon constantly, throughout day and night, to cater for the men of the household (cooking for them, washing for them, beating their dirty clothes, etc.) as they left for and returned from different shifts. Their labour was an essential adjunct before the installation of pit showers and laundries (see Szurek.1985). House cleaning and washing was a relentless physical struggle, without the aid of labour saving devices, against the unhygienic and filthy conditions of the colliery rows, and the dirt (brought in by working miners and the smoggy air) of the pits. Domestic budgeting was particularly problematic given both the size and constant fluctuations in miner's pay. Many women had to find ways of supplementing the household income by, for example, washing, cleaning, and sowing for better-off families. Moreover, whilst maintenance of the harmony and stability of family relations was the primary responsibility of women, it was invariably they who took the wrath, on the grounds of budgeting errors, for cut-backs that had to be made in the pocket money they distributed to the members of the family when the wages brought in fell below usual levels. Shopping for the provisions to fulfil the family's needs and tastes was a particularly onerous task, not merely because of the need to maintain a tight budget, but also because of the unusually poor range of choices brought about by the limited consumer facilities. Finally, on top of all this were the matters of attending to the needs of relatives beyond the home and, to an extent, the needs of the wider community.

The dangers of pit work

Perhaps the greatest uncertainty of all was that posed by a constant threat of death. As in most pits, there was, in comparison to other types of workplace, a high potential for injury and death. Men were injured and lost through roof falls, flooding, gas poisoning, machinery accidents, explosions, caused usually by sparks generated in the hewing process igniting gas, and blood poisoning, resulting from rats urine entering the body through lacerations in the skin. The men I worked with reported an intimate awareness of these dangers, having seen serious accidents, having been injured themselves, or having lost friends, and so on. Nevertheless, they explained that, leaving themselves open to danger was necessary to a degree (for example, because of the heat, men discarded protective clothing to work only in their underpants and boots), and that excessive caution was both unfeasible, unproductive, and, in any case, no guarantee of protection anyway.

The majority of illnesses were, however, of a progressive nature. Most common were stress, deafness, skin problems caused by incessant laceration and contact with oils and dust, arthritis, and, most seriously, silicosis and other forms of pneumoconiosis. The persistent failure of statistics adequately to take account of these has served drastically to under-represent the actual extent of mining related illness and death.

In much of the historical context lived through by the people I worked with, the dangers of the pit were no less severe for dependent women. In their role as carers, it was women who picked up the burden of nursing men disabled for life by the conditions of pit work. Moreover, because of the meagre pensions given to the widows of miners by the coal companies up until nationalization, and the threat of eviction which the tied housing system entailed, a husband's death represented, not only an emotional loss, but an almost total loss of security.

Memories of the fear of impending death are no less

potent for women than for men. They were reminded of the potential of death not merely by the not infrequent major accidents in the area (for example, thirteen men died in one incident at Woodhorn pit in 1916), but by individual deaths which were a regular occurrence. The images of the terror struck by the sound of the pit accident siren, and women leaving their homes to wait together at the pit gates to hear the news of injuries and fatalities and the names of the maimed and dead, are indelibly printed in the collective consciousness of the women residents of the area.

Williamson (1982:118-125) points to the significance of the household routines, which were a part of women's 'compulsive domesticity' (see also, Rosser and Harris:1965), with respect to the psychological burden engendered by having to live with the constant threat of mining death without being able to see or experience work in the pit itself. He argues, with reference to Davidoff (1974), that such routines were a means of avoiding the consequent anxiety of this burden. Immersion in routines, "took the sting away"(1982:126).

The situation facing women I have described is indicative of their almost total dependence on men (brought about primarily because of the low potential for employment and the necessity of the role of the full-time miner's wife). Under such circumstances, pressures on both men and women for early marriage are understandable. Moreover, women I worked with characterized their children as both an insurance policy against the constant high risk of emotional loss and financial ruin. This must in part explain the high degree of value placed upon family life in mining communities which other writers have noted. For example, Williamson (1982:118) emphasizes an importance attached to personal value which is engendered in part by living with the uncertainty of financial rewards.

Being Trapped

The chances of escaping this incessant hardship were minimal. Temporary respite from the conditions faced was barely possible. Up until the Second World War most of the coal companies refused to grant paid holidays. Moreover, the miner's six day week and the incessant domestic work of the miner's wife allowed little free time. However, again with reference to Davidoff (1974), Williamson (1982:120) points out that women created freedom through the strict control and manipulation of their domestic routines. Two underlying implications of Williamson's argument are, that such control and manipulation were a matter of individual organization, and, secondly, that much of women's work, in contrast to the work of men, was extremely isolating (1982:120). However, I found that a great deal of women's work was done collectively (particularly washing and decorating). Secondly, women often organized for their routines to coincide to this end and to make time for various collective tasks in the wider community (for example, organization of charity events, etc.). What is important to emphasize is that in the collective organization of domestic work and in the organization of free time from this work, women built resilient and flexible social networks around the domestic sphere. Male social networks on the other hand tended to focus around the workplace in, for example, the clubs and the allotments, the majority of which were concentrated near to the pits. This is an important point to emphasize as it has considerable bearing on the experience of ageing. I will discuss later how gender differences in the nature of social networks affects the extent to which men and women, respectively, are able to maintain contact with these networks in old age.

Concerning the long term, the lack of occupational diversity and the limits placed, both from above and below, on occupational mobility are perhaps most important in this respect. Entrapment informs the common image of mining people, encapsulated perfectly in the local song, 'Once a miner always a miner, nee way up an' nee way oot', as a marginalized and unequally oppressed section of the working class, and mining itself as a job for life. This latter point was manifest in the fact that during the depression of the nineteen thirties, when there was a substantial degree of out migration from the area many of the migrants did not seek alternative occupations within the U.K. and Europe, but travelled to find work in mining as far afield as South Africa, the

U.S.A. and Canada, where poor pay and working conditions made for an experience often worse than that from which they were escaping. It is perhaps no coincidence that Ashington, like the modern day black British population, for whom the sporting world is one of the few arenas in which success can be achieved, was noted for the production of a succession of sporting heroes; Jackie Milburn, the Charlton brothers, and so on.

Finally, retirement could rarely be described as a well-deserved reward for a working life. The potential for secure retirement was low. Up until shortly before nationalization, the reward for retiring miners was usually one pound from the union and a certificate of service from the company. There was widespread resentment of the A.C.C's compulsory retirement age of seventy. Few were able to accrue enough savings to survive adequately in retirement, and those who could not be supported by their family had to find ways of continuing their working life in some way (largely on the margins of the economy, in part-time menial work) in order to stave off the threat of ending life in one of the work houses.

Having said this, longevity was rare, particularly amongst men. As one seventy eight year old woman explained to me,

"*Owld then and owld now are two different things. If you were as owld as I am now you were really owld. And a man o' my age was really, really owld....owld owld.. ..somebody really special.*"

Gordon calculates that the death rate in Ashington town, with both men, women and children counted together, was, over the period of the twenties, thirties, and forties, often as high as 40% above the national average, and 2% higher at its lowest level (1954:55). Death rates were high not merely because of the strenuousness and, in the case of most men, the danger of working life. Survival on meagre incomes and poor living conditions made for an unhealthy life generally, and lay behind an unusually high rate of epidemics (typhoid, smallpox) which periodically affected the area up until as late as the nineteen fifties (1954:44).

Symbolic Events

The period from the general strike of 1926 to the depression of the nineteen thirties, which terminated with the onset of the preparations for war, was of particular significance to the present day elderly of Ashington. The costs inflicted by both events proceeded in an unrelenting flow. In addition to the wage suppression mentioned earlier, the intervening period of maximum productivity in the pits and relatively high employment was not sufficiently sustained for the people of the area to recover from the first event in preparation for the hardships brought on by the second.

These were the formative years of most of the people I worked with (for the sixty year olds whom I worked with in the clubs in 1986-7 the years 1926-39 were those from birth to the age of thirteen, and over the same period the oldest person was between thirty seven and fifty). Images of the dramatic events of this period are constantly drawn upon to symbolize these elements of hardship which are the constant feature in the self descriptions of their lives.

Memories of the strike consist primarily of, firstly, the dramatic consequences of the A.C.C. evictions. Victims set up homes, furniture and all, in a series of paths between rows in the Hirst. The area came to be known as 'Alley City'. Others formed camps on the slag heaps, risking the ill effects of the sulphur fumes to catch the warmth from the smouldering embers of bastard coal. Secondly, the strike is remembered as a particularly bitter struggle. The success of the action demanded on a community wide scale, the enforcement of a militant solidarity internally, and the virtual isolation and physical defence of the area from the entry of groups of miners from nearby areas who were enticed by the A.C.C. to work in its pits. People I worked with remembered massed battles on the borders of their communities, and the burning of the homes of men who continued to work. Their families were sent to coventry, and rubbish and excrement was thrown at their feet as they passed by in the street. The life of the strike breakers was so intolerable that some were reported to have committed suicide. The extent to which the bitter divisions from this period have persisted through generations is evidenced by the continuing prefixing of the family names of strike breakers; 'The Scab Scott's', etc.

However, the overriding memory of the whole period is that of poverty. One man remembered the contrast between the mass of workers expectantly running to the pit at the rare sound of the work buzzer, with the majority of that same group meandering back dejectedly, having found that they were not among the lucky few to have been drawn in the cavel. Almost all of the people I worked with recounted instances of starvation, the queue for the workhouse, and the ingenious and desperate lengths to which people went to survive. For example, Pegswoodonians remember 'the day of the fish'. Word was passed throughout the village that people should go to the river Wansbeck wear at early morning. In a carefully co-ordinated exercise, a group of men had broken into the pit and stolen all the necessary equipment to cause a series of explosions which would kill enough fish to feed the whole village. One man described the ensuing scene as like, "oot o' the Bible"; scores of men, women and children diving into the water, regardless of whether they could swim or not, to scramble to collect the trout and salmon which floated to the surface.

CONTINUITY AND CHANGE

Significant changes

The most significant changes pointed to by the people I worked with, include the rise of welfarism, relative postwar prosperity, and a series of social and ideological changes which have, in part, been documented by other writers; for example, changes in the organization of leisure (most notably, privatism and the breakdown of single gender socializing practices), changing notions of gender and the organization of marriage (see, for example, Szurek (1985)). Perceptions of such changes by the elderly are outlined in Part II, Section 2, and the relationship of such changes to two central interrelated issues, i.e. the composition of the elderly as a social category, and the relationship between the elderly and other generations are discussed below. As I have made mining central to this historical account, it is appropriate to offer a slightly more detailed summary of the condition of the local mining industry in the critical postwar years and the consequences of changes in this respect at the level of employment.

The organization of mining has undergone considerable changes, brought about primarily by the 'three ations' (a term used by Dennis Murphy, the last Northumberland N.U.M. general secretary); nationalization, rationalization, and technological innovation. Improved pay deals and conditions in the industry worked out in the spirit of corporatism by the state management and the increasingly solidaristic mining unions served to improve pay and conditions in the pits and placed the miners on a comparatively equal financial footing with other manual professions in the post-war years of relative prosperity. However, the benefits of changes in the mining industry were short lived. The Ashington area succumbed to the problem which had afflicted most other parts of the Northumberland coalfield since the nineteen thirties; diminishing coal stocks. Moreover, prompted by the poor export prices for coal and a domestic market which was becoming heavily reliant on cheaper imported coal, the N.C.B. eventually decided against investment in the development of the area's pits which would have enabled the mining of the considerable stocks of deep sea coal. The sixties, seventies and eighties saw the rapid closure of pits throughout the area. In what was seen by many of the people I worked with as the final struggle to protect mining jobs, the old union divisions of the past came back. Their reappearance was to serve in the miners' defeat. Shortly after I left the field, Ashington pit itself was to close, leaving Ellington pit (with only six hundred jobs and a very uncertain future) as the only working non-privatized mine in the whole of Northumberland. As an essentially one industry area the major consequence of this has been, of course, considerable unemployment. Little has come in to replace mining, and the working population is now largely a commuting one, working in Newcastle or in the large light industrial estates which have developed around Cramlington, to the south of the area. Two further facts which are, in part a consequence of the industry's run-down, should also be mentioned. First, at a demographic level, the search for work has prompted a relatively high degree of outmigration. Secondly, the declining significance of the coal industry has contributed to the general trend towards an increase in the number of women as a proportion of the waged working population (Abercrombie. 1988: 124).

Impressions of change

My image of Ashington as a child was as a boring and grey industrial town. Negative feelings towards the place were exacerbated by the fact that every Sunday (the most depressing of days) we had to perform the onerous task of visiting my grandfather (though I loved him very much, he used to spend the whole afternoon discussing political questions of which I had no understanding). All the way to and from his house in the Hirst rows my mother and father would pass critical comments about the place, glad that they had escaped to the environmentally more pleasant town of Morpeth. I agreed and felt blessed that they had.

In my eight year absence from the area after my grandfather's death these images were fortified by time and stereotypical black and white media images of mining communities. When I returned in the winter of 1986, initial impressions were as if time had stood still. The images and stereotypes were reinforced. The seemingly endless rows of colliery houses with their curious little corner sweet shops were still there. The pit head machinery was still the dominating feature of the skyline. The air was still muggy and smelt of coal burning fires, and the sky still teemed with flocks of racing pigeons.

However, initial impressions soon eroded with familiarity. All around, the visible symbols of change soon became evident. Whilst the growth of some of the villages, such as Linton, Lynemouth, and Newbiggin, has reversed, the peripheries of others have pushed outward with housing developments. These have served to alter radically the structural nature of different communities. To give polarized examples; whilst Bothal and West Ashington have been progressively proletarianized by extensive council house building, the reverse has occurred in Ellington, where up-market private houses, built to accommodate the comparatively enriched younger mining people who lived/live from the village's pit, now outnumber the rows. The objects of a dynamic consumer capitalism which are evident in every street (from satellite dishes to D.I.Y. alterations to the rows) break past monotony and uniformity. Evidence of changing social habits is everywhere. One of Ashington's first working men's club, 'The Seaton', has now gone. In its place, near to what remains of a pit slag heap, stands a dischoteque. Surreally, a mooted name for this establishment was Manhattan Skyline. Its clientele, like that in most of the other pubs and clubs, including the working men's clubs, is increasingly becoming a mix of young men and women, dressed in styles which contradict the image of cloth cap and braces.

Finally, and most importantly, most of the visible symbols of mining are little more than a facade. The gigantic slurry pond at the back of Woodhorn pit is still there, but it has been cleaned and dredged for the windsurfers who use it. The slag heap which stretched much of the length of Ashington town from Ashington pit to Woodhorn pit is slowly being landscaped. Of those pits left (Ashington, Ellington, Lynemouth, and Woodhorn) Lynemouth and Ashington are just a mass of derelict buildings, and Woodhorn has been turned into a heritage museum manned by one of the last generations of retired miners, whose numbers are being rapidly caught up by the coal figurines of hewers which adorn shop windows of the area and which no doubt will soon become the relics of a mining past that has finally disappeared.

Change and the constitution of the social category of the elderly

The post war years have seen an increased potential for a degree of financial stability in old age. In addition to overall wage rises, nationalization in mining saw the introduction of incremental pay structures and pay according to length of service rather than pay exclusively according to productivity and the nature of employment. As implied before, movement of many of the elderly pit workers to datal duties entailed wage reduction prior to retirement. The restructuring of the industry, most notably with respect to the implementation of more meritocratic recruitment, training and promotion procedures, enhanced the potential of ordinary miners to achieve safer and better paying grades in the pits. Finally, and perhaps of greatest importance have been the introduction of statutory state and occupational pensions.

It is, however, important to note that these benefits did not come about as an immediate and unrelenting change. This is reflected in the scepticism shown towards nationalization and welfarism by many of the people I worked with. One man commented on nationalization in the mining industry,

"The only changes Aa seen in me day waz that the same fyeces who med aall the decisions afore waz sittin' ahind the same desks, except noo the' hed shiny new name plates with a new job description."

The fact is, I was told, that, despite the restructuring of the industry, the nepotistic aspects of recruitment and promotion procedures and the aspects of the employment structure which served to act as a disincentive to promotion persisted long after nationalization. Moreover, the size of occupational pensions and redundancy payments have varied vastly, according to grades and, importantly, through time, up to the present day.

The important point to make here is that the modern day elderly are far from being a homogeneous social category. Differences of wealth which previously cross-cut the elderly at the level of class have become increasingly existent at a cross-generational level. People I worked with stressed such difference by the operation of categories such as the old old and the new old, and many of those who considered themselves of the former characterized themselves as being of a forgotten generation overlooked by many of the beneficial changes of recent years.

Having said this, such categories are not merely informed by financial differences according to age. The elderly have become a more heterogeneous category in other than financial respects, throughout the age ranges, as a consequence of other changes, particularly those of a sociological and ideological nature outlined above. The significance of such heterogeneity is followed up later in the book (see, particularly Part III, Section 3 on 'association and conflict').

Change and the relationship of the elderly to younger generations

The social category 'old aged' is a relative concept (see, for example, Cowgill and Holmes (1978:14-28)). Amongst the people I worked with I found chronological ageing to be of little significance as a definitive criterion of old aged. Selection of self descriptive categories seemed to be dependent on particular contexts. For example, the concept of generation, defined largely by participation in such contexts as the clubs for the elderly was salient when people expressed commonality or criticism of younger age groups. Old age was salient when the problems of physiological ageing were confronted. Nevertheless, it should be pointed out that, particularly in the case of men, retirement from waged work is considered to be a significant criterion.

Given this ambiguity it is difficult to talk specifically about the size of the elderly as a social category other than to say that not only has it grown considerably, but also that it has grown disproportionately in relation to other generational categories. Ashington is, quite literally, an area that is ageing. The number of those facing permanent retirement from waged labour has grown as a result of lower statutory retirement ages and increasing levels of redundancy in an area of high unemployment. Life expectancy has increased dramatically, although, despite the boasts of the N.C.B. and B.C., this has had little to do with post-nationalization improvements in the conditions of mining work. Finally, the cross-generational ratio has been affected by post-war birth rates which have been consistently lower than in the first part of this century, and the out migration of younger inhabitants in search of work.

The disproportionate growth of a largely state dependent elderly population is a significant factor in lowering of the status of the elderly with respect to other age groups. However, this lowering of status should also be seen in the context of the other changes outlined. Increasing cross-generational incomes fissures, the run-down of the mining industry and technical changes in the mining which have made old forms of working knowledge obsolete, changes in the organization of recruitment to the industry which have undermined the element of nepotism which existed, and the assumption by the state of roles which had previously been carried out by ordinary members of the community, have served to disrupt the relations of power and interdependence between young and old.

3-PEOPLE, CONTEXTS, AND MEANS OF CONTACT

The starting point for my fieldwork was a series of clubs for the elderly. Though most of these were women dominated, through meeting people within them, they provided a means of gaining contact with both elderly women and men in other contexts.

Darby and Joan, and Over 55s clubs

On arrival in Ashington I was put into contact, through Age Concern and the Women's Royal Voluntary Service, with a number of clubs for the elderly. My choice of working in four of these was based on geographical convenience. I was accepted without any problems into all four by their respective organizers. First, I will highlight a series of key features and problems which were common to all four, and then outline the nature of each club separately in so far as they each had unique characteristics.

Officially, the clubs are intended for the use of anyone over the age of fifty five. In reality the organizers of such clubs often discouraged Social Services from providing transport for potential participants. The intention, which is explicitly recognized as such, by club organizers, umbrella organizations (i.e. Age Concern and W.R.V.S.), and Social Services alike, is to restrict their use, as far as possible, to 'the more active elderly' (Northumberland Health Authority, Social Services, and Community Health Council.1986:26). However, the extent to which this intention can be fulfilled varies greatly according to their proximity to the homes of the type of elderly people whom they wished not to encourage. Reflecting their more common participation in community roles, and their attachment to such organizations, all the clubs were run by women. With few exceptions they are run on co-operative principles, not in the specific ways in which the working men's clubs are organized, but in the sharing of tasks, responsibilities and decisions. Finally, the leaders of all the clubs claimed that they were having problems with maintaining their membership levels. This was explained in a number of ways; people are reluctant to join such clubs because it is tantamount to self identification as elderly, changing socializing habits, etc.

Ellington Darby and Joan club - As the name states the club is situated in Ellington. This is the biggest of the clubs I worked in, with approximately sixty members attending each weekly meeting. There are a number of reasons for its relative popularity. It is one of the few social alternatives in what is an area with very limited facilities. The provision of club entertainment (concert parties, amateur plays, etc.) was always consistent and often of high quality, and the organizers rarely had to fall back on the last resort activities such as bingo. The club leader was an exceptionally affable and popular woman. Finally, the club offered members the chance to participate in a range of activities which other clubs did not offer. Most importantly, it had a choir and a touring concert party. The age range of the membership was very wide, and there were only marginally more women than men. Most of those who attended came from Lynemouth and Ellington. They were predominantly, but not all, mining people.

Northumberland Close over 55's club - This club is situated in Bothal and draws its membership from that area and West Ashington. Participants were from a variety of occupational backgrounds; mining and other working class people, and middle class people of mining management and other professional or business backgrounds. There was an average weekly attendance rate of around fifty. Members of all ages from fifty five and upwards were represented, but the majority of members were of the upper age ranges. This is largely explained by the fact that the club is situated in a sheltered home for the elderly from where it draws most of its membership. Despite this fact, again, the number of women participants was only marginally more than the number of men. Again, the large and mixed membership can, in part be explained by the fact that this particular area offers few social alternatives and is badly serviced by public transport to other areas. Despite the large number of participants, when I arrived at the club it was in a state of considerable decline. The club leader explained that almost no new younger members were joining. People I spoke to who went from club to club explained, unfairly perhaps, this decline as resulting from the bad reputation the club had developed. The club offered little in the way of entertainment. Every week was one long bingo session which members frequently complained about. Moreover, the meetings were riddled with disagreements and arguments between members.

Oakville Darby over 55's club - This club is situated in the north part of Hirst. Its members were almost exclusively mining people from the colliery rows in that area. On average there was an attendance rate of around thirty five. However, there were only four regular male participants. It is feasible to speculate that the disparity may in part be explained by a working class traditionalism concerning gender differentiated socializing practices. What is clear is that the disparity can largely be accounted for by the area's proximity to a range of social and leisure arenas, including the working men's clubs, in the centre of Ashington. The age range in the club was relatively wide, but as in the case of the Northumberland Close club, there was a disproportionately high number from the upper age ranges, largely because of its situation next to an old people's home and a sheltered housing complex. The atmosphere in the club was friendly, and people were generally happy with the way the club was run. Though the club leader was very firm in laying down the rules of the W.R.V.S. (for example, she tried not to allow alcohol on the premises), she is a highly respected local charity worker who people were careful not to criticize. Moreover, although not a wealthy club, the organizers made sure that there was some modest form of entertainment at least every fortnight.

Hirst Darby and Joan club - This club is situated in the south part of the Hirst. All its members were mining people from the surrounding colliery rows. There were only fifteen regular members. They were all of a similar age; in their late sixties and early seventies. Moreover, there were only three male members, and these left within two months of the commencement of my fieldwork. The reason for these facts lies not only in its location, i.e. near to a range of other social and leisure alternatives. The club leader had set up the club only six months prior to my arrival, under the auspices of the W.R.V.S. She had invited her friends and informed a number of other enquirers that the club was full. Apparently, the club drew very heavily on her informal female social network that she had participated in for a number of years. Whilst she did not actively discourage the participation of men, the club became identified as one for women and developed an ambience unconducive to male participation.

Age Concern Luncheon Club Day Centres

As the term suggests the luncheon clubs provide a meal and are run during the day time rather than in the evening as is the case with the type above. They also provide entertainment. They cater specifically for elderly people who are living in their own home, and acceptance is dependent on recommendation by health or Social Service staff. Though transport is organized to bring participants to the clubs, the informal rules of membership state that they must be sufficiently mobile to make their own way. The clubs cater for people suffering from a range of problems; isolation, depression brought on by widowhood, etc.

I initially attended two of these clubs. However,

because of transport difficulties I had to give up attending one of these. The club I attended, the Ellington day centre, had about thirty members. They were from a variety of backgrounds and came from Ellington, Lynemouth, and the smaller mining villages to the north of the Ashington area. All except one of the official members were women. However, three men, who it was explained to me, were widowers, turned up each week to take advantage of the cooked meal. Mrs. Howie, the club leader, got around any objections which A.C. might have raised on the premise that they had not been sent by the Social Services by claiming that they were helpers. Again the participants were of a wide age range, but most were in their late seventies or early eighties.

Working Men's clubs and 'The Buffs'

I spent a considerable amount of time working in a number of the area's working men's clubs, but two, The Linton and Woodhorn, which is near to Woodhorn pit, and The Progressive, which is close to Ashington pit, became my regulars. The former one is used almost exclusively by elderly men, most of whom are retired miners. The latter, also, is used predominantly by elderly men and ex-miners, but because of its proximity to what was then a working pit it was a stop-off place for working miners going to and from their shifts.

I also became a member of 'The Buffs', 'The Royal Antediluvian Order of the Buffaloes'. One man I spoke to described the organization as 'a poor man's Masons'. Like the Masons it involves a set of formal initiation rituals. The organization has its own club and a number of lodges within the club. The lodge I joined was on the verge of folding. It had only twelve members, all of whom, with the exception of myself, were over seventy. However, occasionally, we were visited by the younger members of another lodge who came specifically to spend money with the intention of keeping our own lodge afloat. Lodge activities consist mainly of talking, drinking, singing, and the raising of money for charity, though because of the precarious financial position of the lodge of which I was a member, most of the money raised had to go into upkeep costs. Fund raising is done by the operation of a mock court, which charges and fines members for minor indiscretions and fabricated accusations of misdemeanours.

Informal contexts

Through participation in these contexts I was introduced to other less formal contexts by club members I became close to. I regularly used to go to the dog races and the allotments with a group of elderly men, Bart, Jim, and George, from the Linton and Woodhorn club. Through one of the women, Hilda (the comedienne) (introduced later), at the Oakville club I was invited to attend women's parties, coffee mornings and shopping trips, and, to a limited degree, some of the women and myself organized to meet in the execution of our domestic tasks. For example, I regularly used to meet with a group of elderly women at the informal social arena of the launderette every Tuesday morning.

Through participation in the clubs I was also invited to people's homes, where I was given the opportunity to record interviews. It should also be pointed out that many such interviews were conducted with people I had never met before. Whilst walking around the streets of Ashington it was not uncommon to be greeted by strangers and questioned about my activities. This frequently led to being invited indoors for tea and a chat.

FOOTNOTES

(1) The close association of Lynemouth, Linton, and Ellington with Ashington is explained by the fact that Ashington is their urban and commercial centre, and by the fact that their development was largely due to the expansion and investment of the Ashington Coal Company. Although Ashington is the commercial and urban centre for Guide Post and Stakeford, their division from Ashington by the river Wansbeck, and their growth as a result of the investment of a different coal company, serves to weaken the association. Similarly, Newbiggin's association with Ashington is weakened, first, because its development is owed to a different coal company, and also because, unlike Ashington, it is an ancient village whose early growth centred upon the fishing industry. Unlike all the other villages, for Pegswood Ashington is not the main urban and commercial centre. Moreover, its growth was largely due to the activities of coal companies other than the A.C.C.. Nevertheless, like the other villages, it was a mining village, and the major facets of its identity were constructed around this central feature. This distinguishes it from the town of Morpeth, with which it is most proximate, and identifies it with Ashington, which was the heart of the mining industry in the area.

PART II
COMMUNITY AND CHANGE

"There are a number of Over 60's Clubs and Darby and Joan type clubs throughout the County. They provide the opportunity for the more active elderly to simply drop in for a chat and meet others or join in the range of activities provided for them -guest speakers, bingo, dominoes, whist, old time sing-along, outings, etc." (Northumberland, Health Authority, Social Services, and Community Health Council.1986:26).

The image portrayed of the elderly participants in these institutions is of passive users enjoying a little unimportant conversation and nostalgic entertainment. In reality I found that they are involved, through conversation and the celebration of local popular culture, of whose construction they actively play a part, in a continuing social commentary about their condition. Central in this is the representation and celebration of an image of local community, and the way in which this is seen to have been subjected to radical change. In this respect they are not engaging in simple nostalgia, as the quote implies, for these images which are celebrated and represented, serve a purpose within their lives.

These points are expanded below. The first section contains a detailed outline and analysis of the features of this community, its relationship to the world beyond its boundaries, and the central referents in its representation (1). The second section contains a discussion of the representations of change.

In both sections I draw on interview and participant observational data. I draw extensively on the local popular culture which I gathered in the process of observation. Additionally, in section 2 much of the data comes from an informal discussion group organized at the suggestion of four women whom I talked with regularly in the Ellington day centre. The issue we decided upon was suitably broad: 'the past and the present - the major differences.'

1-THE REPRESENTATION AND CELEBRATION OF COMMUNITY: POINTS OF REFERENCE

Three points of reference pervade the representation and celebration of community in the social contexts in which I worked. These are, a north-south relation, the area as consisting of distinct communities, and the mining life (defined in relevant subsection). The significance of each of these in the representation of community is different. I shall deal with each in turn.

The north-south relation

A perceived north-south relation is important to the representation of community in two related senses. An extract from an interview with a man I spoke with regularly gives a sense of these.

"*Aa've seen a canny bit o' the world. Aa left Ashington wi me fatha to gan to Pittsburg when there waz ney work left here for wuz, but the' treated wuz like slaves, so Aa med me way back an' ended up in London in Islington, working for a Jewish family, forniture polishin' Aa waz. Mind, Aa waz nivver see happy as when me Motha giz the call to get hyem. The Noose needed fillin'. Ya cannat beat the folks up here man. They'll give ya the time o' day. There's a spirit o' community. Talk tuv a stranger doon sooth an' the look in their eyes is like ya ganna murder them. Mind it's nee surprise wat with aall them drugs, an' muggings, an' the bairns bein' molested. Aa wadn't send one o' me own doon theyor. Ya might think nout tuv it noo, but give it fifty yors an' you'll be able to draw a line sooth o' Middlesbrough. The sooth'll not be fit for gannin'; the dangers, an' there'll be nee clean air or green fields. Then we'll be dein' the laughin' instead o' them. It'll sorve them right for aall the yors they've been mekin' use o' the money we med for them.*" (2).

(i) The account typifies the representation of community in exaggerated critical juxtaposition in the context of a north-south relation. In his book, 'The Symbolic Construction of Community', Cohen points to this process. He states that individuals, 'define themselves by reference to a 'significant other'; likewise, 'self-conscious' cultures and communities. Moreover, just as other cultures are only observable from the perspective of a culture with which it is contrasted, so also people see their own culture from the supposed vantage point at which they imagine others to view it. Since the vitality of cultures lies in their juxtaposition, they exaggerate themselves and each other.' (Cohen.1985:115).

Two points should be drawn from this. Firstly, the point of reflexive exaggeration and the exaggeration of the other, and secondly, the imagined view by the other and its exaggeration; the putative image.

Reflexive exaggeration and the exaggeration of the other: In the case of this cultural context where the south is represented as a significant other culture, the ability to sustain exaggeration (it is justifiable to suggest that accounts are frequently of moral panic proportions (Cohen.1972)) is easily facilitated. It is amenable to fiction. It is a distant reality, whose images are available largely as sensational media fragments, and though many such descriptions are fuelled by experience, factual accountability is unimportant; devices such as the use of the future are used to overcome this problem. The outcome of this exaggerated juxtaposition is the generation of a multiplicity dichotomies; moral (for example, S-N = immoral-moral), social (for example, S-N = social atomism-community), and, in direct contradistinction to typical southern stereotypes of the north, environmental (for example, S-N. = polluted ecological desert - clean rural wilderness), etc. These serve to establish an idealized, essential difference between North and South.

The imagined view by the other: Whilst exaggerated, putative images of, in this case, the north by the southern other, are central to the celebration and representation of community, they are, of course selectively built around facts (there is such a thing as a negatively stereotypical image of the north). The manner in which the implicit negative connotations are exaggerated but transformed as part of the positive representation of locality will be clarified later.

(ii)The north-south relation is also central to the representation of community in what can be loosely defined as its political aspect. This is fuelled by a regional socialist political discourse which has developed through years of political domination in the area by the Labour Party and The National Union of Mineworkers.

The relation is characterized as an exploitative one. Central to this are, firstly, the idea that the profits of the south are quite literally fuelled by the labour of the north, and, secondly, the explanation of economic slumps, not as crises of capital, but as *ad hoc* exploitation of north by south. As one man told me, *"the' might hev nee use for wuz now , but they'll come back for more when it teks their fancy an' the' hey a need of it"*.

In addition, there is a perception of regional state favouritism. Southerners are widely regarded as being the main beneficiaries of government policy. As one man stated in explanation of the employment crisis, "*there's nee jobs for the bairns.... southerners has got aall the jobs....that lot doon at Westminster sees t' that*". In explaining why she had had to queue for an E.E.C. butter hand-out to pensioners, a woman told me, "*nee doot the' let them doon sooth tek aall the' wanted an' left the scraps for us lot up here*".

This political aspect of perceptions of the north-south relation plays a part in explaining the hardships which themselves are central referents in common explanation of community internal features. It also informs the characterization of features of community whose definition arises from perceptions of its relationship to the world beyond its boundaries. For example, specific features are represented as a manifestation of autonomy in relation to the state, necessitated by state neglect.

Finally, it should be pointed out that the geographical boundaries demarcating north and south are vague, generally arbitrary, and largely unimportant. The south begins anywhere between south of the river Tyne and Watford Gap service station (London's northern most point), or it doesn't begin at any particular place at all. This is partially the case because the relation is primarily a juxtapositional mechanism. However, the vagueness relates to the perceived exploitative aspect of the relation. The south is essentially a convenient metaphor to encapsulate a set of vaguely defined agencies which are seen to have exploited the area. This vagueness is not surprising. With the privatisation of the coal industry and consequent cessation of the A.C.C., the perceived agencies of exploitation (for example, the state, capital) have become less visible, and visible primarily as located in the south.

Local Communities

According to the poetry and song that form the backbone of entertainment in the clubs for the elderly and the humour and reminiscences generated amongst the participants in these contexts the local area comprises a distinct set of communities whose boundaries and names are often different to those presented in official geography. Most of the isolated villages surrounding the town of Ashington itself keep their names (i.e. Ellington, Lynemouth, Linton, Newbiggin and Pegswood), and their perceived boundaries are the same as official boundaries. However, with the exception of Woodbridge, in the case of the constituent areas of the town of Ashington, and the outlying villages of Stakeford and Guide Post, alternative names are used and official boundaries disregarded.

Hirst and North Seaton is referred to as 'The East End'. Within this area there is a small enclave which is not officially recognised, which is referred to as 'Chinatown'. West Ashington and Bothal are referred to as 'High Market'. And, finally, Stakeford and Guide Post are referred to collectively, by some more radically orientated people at least, as 'Scabtown'.

Each community and its inhabitants are represented as possessing distinct characteristics. The native community is of course usually positively represented. I shall refer here only to the views of the outsider. The name High Market probably derives from the former class composition of the area. Reflecting this, its inhabitants are referred to either deferentially as, for example, 'classy', or of 'good stock', or critically as 'The Toffs', 'The Snobs', and so on. The inhabitants of Scabtown, referred to as, 'The Scabs From Ower the Wettor', derive their name, I was told, from an event in the nineteen thirties when scab labour was brought in from that area to man Woodhorn and Ashington collieries whose men were on strike. A confrontation occurred between the massed ranks of the two sets of workers, on the bridge connecting the two areas, and, it was suggested to me, resentment between the people of the areas simmered for some years. Lynemouth is noted pejoritavely by many people frtom other villages at least for its people's violence and hedonism. People referred to it variously as, 'The Wild West', 'Cannibal Country', and so on. The people from Pegswood are referred to by some people as 'The Treacle Ponders'. The name derives from the pit slurry pond which was the central landmark of the village. However, the prevailing identity which Pegswoodonians are attributed with is not one of uncleanliness. Rather, they are renowned for (unfairly, of course) a lack of intelligence. The people of Newbiggin are renowned for their superstition. In the case of Ellington and Linton their rural isolation is the source of their identity. They are referred to variously as 'country bumpkins', 'potato heads', and so on, and the suggestion that they speak a rural form of Northumbrian rather than 'the Pitmatic' is a source of humour. The name Chinatown derives from the fact that the low quality housing which once predominated in the area gave the area the appearance of a shanty town. It was considered a no-go area for many, the old location for Ashington's most deprived, and an area of rampant crime and sin apparently. I found little data surrounding the identification of the Eastenders.

A number of points should be made about this. Occasionally people refer to the identities in the explanation of events, or events were pointed to as verification of the identities. One woman told me that it was perhaps not surprising that her sister-in-law had become slovenly in her role as a housewife when she moved to Lynemouth. No doubt she had been sucked into the club life up there, like all the other women in the village, and had forgotten about her duties. Another woman told me that the children of Pegswood had had a history of educational underachievement. When I asked her if the school there had a bad reputation she said that it was nothing to do with this. She explained, suggesting an inherent characteristic, that, "*they've always hed a reputation.... not a brainy stock they've nivver hed nee wit runnin' in theyor blood."*

Having said this, as stated at the outset, these identities are largely mere sources of humour. In most cases, since their inception this has probably been so. High Market and Scabtown are exceptions. Nevertheless, the factors which informed their identities have diminished in significance through time. The 'high class' enclave which was High Market has been substantially eroded by council house developments in the area. And, whilst earlier I emphasized that community divisions from the strike of 1926 have carried through to the present, there are fewer and fewer people who can recall the actual event which gave Scabtown its name. Secondly, the high extent of mobility within the A.C.C. area has obviously militated against the type of insularity and localism which would foster rigid community identities. Thirdly, as they are all northern mining communities, each of them falls within the scope of the referents of the north-south relation and the mining life, such that what constitutes their commonality outweighs in significance what constitutes their differences. Finally, it could be suggested that the proximity of each community to one another makes them less amenable to the type of exaggerated juxtaposition which characterizes the descriptions of the north-south relation, i.e. exaggerated identities in this context are more open to empirical refutation.

Having said this, the construction of negative

identities and the process of critical Juxtaposition at this geographical level is continuous. When a locality displays some specific features which are relevant in the present, these are seized upon and exaggerated. It is in this sense that Woodbridge is currently relevant.

The mining life

By the mining life I am referring to all aspects of life both within, i.e. organizational aspects (for example, the cavel, the division of labour, etc.), the nature of pit work (for example, the drudgery and danger), and the exigencies of pit work (for example, the necessity of adherence to general codes of safety), and outside the pit, at least as they are seen to relate to the industry (for example, the constant threat of the death of working family members, the insecurity of income, affecting both mining people and those not directly associated with the industry).

In the explanation of the features of the community, overt reference is continually made to pit work and the lifestyle which is seen to be peculiar to mining areas. Moreover, symbolism surrounding the nature of pit work (which is often unconsciously intertwined in such explanations) informs the representation of the features of community. Such symbolism usually concerns the inherent potential of mining death, and coal itself. There are a number of reasons why coal should be imbued with a 'symbolic load' (Douglas, 1966:3). Of greatest importance is the problematic dependence on the substance, i.e. the unpredictability and uncertainty brought about by the nature of largely external market. Coal is seen as analogous to, and is attributed with, human qualities. It is both good and evil, but must be treated well if the former quality is to become manifest. The creaking and grinding of earth movement is commonly represented as the coal speaking to indicate its strength or weakness. Similarly, adherence to safety procedures is represented in terms of appeasing the coal.

Another symbolic attribute of coal was its powers of protection, evidenced by the crust of coal which they allowed to collect on their back until the end of the week's shift when it could then, and only then, be washed away. When I asked what the significance of this practice was it was explained that it was believed that, "*if ya washed ya back ya thowt ya would weaken*". The suggestion is that the coal provides a protective crust on the back, the usual point of contact between the miner and the earth above him, i.e. that which must be prevented from collapse. Coal is then, I would suggest imbued with the symbolic power of protection. However, what is important to emphasize here, in the context of the discussion of community, is that, firstly, coal plays a part in the rituals which symbolize the represented and celebrated features of community, and, secondly, it directly symbolizes these features, community identity, and the community's relationship to the world beyond its boundaries (3).

Finally, as this emphasis on boundary implies, the centrality of the mining identity plays a role in the demarcation of the area in the local geographical context. The juxtaposition of the cluster of mining communities to non-mining communities is facilitated by the area's proximity to predominantly rural communities to the north- west and west, and a market town, Morpeth, to the south west. Morpeth is highly significant, particularly with respect to the putative identity of the area. In many ways Morpeth is the antithesis to Ashington. It is a commercial centre with little industry (its most famous product, the 'Barber' jacket, which is a sartorial requirement of the upper classes, is one with considerably more status than coal). Its working classes are resident in the outer parts of the town. Its centre is dominated by fancy shops, bookshops, hunting and fishing shops, and the smart flats and houses of Newcastle office commuters. Like Ashington, Morpeth can legitimately claim, as the birth and burial place of the suffragette Emily Davison, a radical heritage. However, this is obliterated; none existent in its tourist pamphlets. It is its ancient historical tradition, the likes of which Ashington can boast virtually none, along with the features outlined above, and its upmarket, semi-rural, quaint image which adds to Morpeth's reputation as a place for Northumbrians to take the day out. Finally, it is, according to my experience, the dream town of aspiring Ashingtonians who are either ashamed of their working class, industrial origins, or who, like my parents did, see out migration to Morpeth as the normal accompaniment to upward occupational mobility. This fact, above all, is central to an excessively negative view of the Ashington area in the local context.

ASHINGTON MEN AND WOMEN: REPRESENTATIONS OF THE SEXUAL DIVISION OF LABOUR AND GENDER IDENTITIES (4)

In this sub-section I will show that an ideal of a rigid sexual division of labour within the family unit is celebrated in the context of the clubs for the elderly and that gender identities relate to this division. I will also show that the pit is central to these ideals. Images of masculinity are inextricably bound with pit work. An ever present threat of mining death informs notions of male identity and serves in the legitimation of certain aspects of male behaviour. As pointed out earlier in the book, this threat has always been great for the women of the area as well as the miners themselves. Other writers have commented on the relationship between this threat and the nature of female relations (for example see Szurek (1985) (5). My interest here, however, is in showing how pit work, and this threat of mining death, inform the stereotypical images of women and give these stereotypes an added power, which legitimizes a rigid sexual division of labour and, ultimately, the control of women.

The celebration and representation of the sexual division of labour

The comedian in 'The Evergreens' concert party told a humorous story about the initial meeting with, and then the marriage to, his wife, and his frustrated expectations about the organization of their marriage. It was unclear whether the story was a fiction or was based on his personal experiences of marriage. It provided a carriage for the usual mother-in-law, and 'her indoors' jokes, but more fundamentally, the humour stems from an inversion of the common ideal. He met his wife at a local dance. After a few meetings at the dance she allowed him to walk her home. On the journey he dropped and lost a very expensive gold watch. He should have realised that this was an omen, because after the marriage he discovered that his wife *"waz nee good"*; she couldn't cook, was a terrible cleaner, and was virtually illiterate. He was particularly angry with her family for not informing him about this beforehand, for he wouldn't have entered the marriage if he had known that she was not in possession of these basic skills. It was clear that they had found her to be a liability around the home and wanted her off their hands. The marriage had been one long nightmare of doing all the chores (cooking, cleaning, sorting out the bills, etc.) which a wife would normally be expected to take care of. They'd got the reputation of being an anti-social couple, as she could not be trusted to help the neighbours. The only time he sent her to baby-sit for Mrs. Brown next door, "*shi varnye chowked the bairn.*" One of the worst things about the marriage was that she couldn't deal with money. He couldn't trust her to do the shopping, and before they came to the club each Wednesday night he had to give her a bag of small change which she would return in portions when he needed it to pay for his bingo cards so that at least they could present the appearance that she was in control of matters financial. Despite all the problems, he had never considered divorce. You just didn't do that sort of thing in the old days.

The ideal which this inverts is of a family unit with a rigid sexual division of labour. Similarly, the image of one or other of the sexes attempting to cross this division is also a source of humour. A stereotypical image of the man as almost totally lacking in practical, domestic and organizational skills is a central celebrated theme.

'War Geordie, ee's a canny lad,
Spite nor greed in ees soul ee nivver had,
To prove ees generosity,
Ee'll offer help whenever needs be.
Ee hord us gripin' on last year,
Aboot me kitchen.... of gadgets an' gimmicks it waz bare,
So Geordie declares aall alood,
"Aa'll mek ya one t' mek ya prood."
With joy an' glee Aa accepted ees offer,
Ee telt us ee'd dee it reet an' proper,
But when Aa retorned t' mek the tea,
Such an aafyull site ya nivver did see.

A claes prop haddin' up the tap,
Drowers lined wey an owld proggy mat,
Ee even used the wheels off wor Doris' bairns pram (a
rotatin' towel rack ee called it), Aa shooted,"away oot o'
my kitchen ya bloody man."
So ladies listen t' wat Aa hey t' say,
A hewin' man's good for pout but ornin' pay,
On matters nivver let him loose,
Or ya'll end up wey a home like Rammy's hoose'.
('Wor Geordie', M. Nattrass: Unpublished).

The ideal celebrated then, is of a rigid sexual division of labour, where the man is responsible for waged labour and the financial sustenance of the family, and the women is responsible for the financial organization in the family, all domestic labour and childcare, and caring and organizational roles in the wider community. The only normal roles for men within the home area were gardening and coal collection; tasks which, it should be added, are outside the house itself.

The celebration and representation of gender

This ideal is partially reflected in the characterization of men's and women's identities. Being a good grandmother, mother, housekeeper, and household peacekeeper are the central virtues pointed to in the celebration and evaluation of women, and the most potent image of the woman is of an all powerful matriarch in complete control of the home.

> 'He pulls the bed-claes ower his heed, (Some minutes mare he'll try), But muthor's voice 'ud wake the deed, And he timidly answers, "Aye". Off cums his linin's, vest, and sark, He strips reet doon t' the buff, Me muthor gi's his arse a yark, And shoots, "Oot nao yuv had enough"'.
> From 'The Foreshift' (Coombs. — —:26).

This matriarchal power is personified by her financial control which she assumes when the wage packet is handed over to her for distribution.

> 'Aa hevn't much use for the women,
> Though often Aa praise their gud luks,
> Aa knaa they've control o' the money,
> So Aa try to keep in their gud byuks'.
> From 'Jack the Coal Man' (Coombs. — —:8).

Similarly the celebrated images of men relate to work, and, almost totally, to pit work. The hardships and inherent dangers of the job, and the attainment of maximum productivity are central in this respect.

> 'It's an honour just to claim,
> The pit crack putter's name,
> For competition flourishes 'mang the best,
> Brute strength is in the runnin',
> Only when combined wi' cunnin'
> And a flair for twinin' better than the rest.
> From 'The Putter-Lad', (author not known).

Descriptions of legendary 'yackers' or 'hewers' fill

the historical accounts of the area and family oral biographies. Moreover, an awareness of the pressure exerted as a consequence of an inability to live up to the reputation and expectations of the family in this respect is cited as a reason for departure from the industry. One man explained to me that his cousin had been seconded into his uncle's stone driving team, but simply could not keep up with the pace of their work. They had tried to carry him through but the shame of not being able to pull his weight had led him to resign from the team and join the ordinary cavel. After some time on the cavel he became the object of ridicule amongst a section of the men, as the reason for his transfer was realised, and though he made enough money to support his family, he decided to escape the shame by moving to another area, where he left mining altogether to join a profession of lesser status. He became a policeman.

Concerning the hardships and dangers of the job, local popular culture and the descriptions of the people I worked with, characterize the occupation of pit work as one of living on the knife edge of life and death, and fuel an image of the miner as the ultimate specimen of masculinity. As one man I spoke to cogently explained, *"There's nee job like it....nee tougher job. When ya gan doon bye ya propin' the whole earth up on ya back"*. (The imagery of the back being the point upon which the earth rests corresponds with the perception of coal as a protective crust).

The critical juxtaposition of gender identities

The nature of the relations of men are a central terrain of celebration. These are seen to be characterized by a series of principles and mores: sociability, honesty, scorn for the love of money, the ability to stand your round, scorn for one-upmanship, financial modesty, etc. In addition to their celebration, they are, in practical terms, the subject of exaggerated overemphasis and enforcement. For example, in the early days of my fieldwork, I made the mistake of asking about the size of the redundancy packages that the men were receiving these days. I got little response and later in the evening one of the men took me to one side and explained that you just don't ask that type of question. He implied that knowledge of the financial means of other men would be a source of friction. I also noticed that in the formal context of the Buffs it is considered quite legitimate to impose fines on men for features of behaviour, such as mild pretentiousness, which might in other social contexts be considered a negative idiosyncrasy, but would by no means be considered a punishable misdemeanour. Despite pointing to the variety of these principles and mores, one overriding feature can be extricated to describe them and the intention of their enforcement. They are characterized by a systematic homogeneity; the men were attempting to stress equality and commonality of condition.

These are critically juxtaposed with a series of

negatively stereotypical characterizations of women. Images of the money grabbing, dishonest, nagging, etc., wife are the subject of celebration and humour.

'A nagging wife promotes the strife, That maims and kills affection, And buries it deep, in lasting sleep, Past hope of resurrection.' From 'The Nagging Wife', (author not known).

Coal, the danger of the pit gender relations

At the outset I noted that the constant threat of death within the pit informed the perceived features of community. The relationship of this threat to gender relations and identities is the theme I will develop here.

MEN

(i) The relationship between the necessity of safety and the principles and mores of male social relations: Despite my emphasis on these mores and principles as a celebrated and practiced feature of male relations, these relations are also complemented by a degree of competitiveness and antagonism. This is not paradoxical. These mores are in themselves counters in antagonistic relations, as I demonstrate later. Moreover, both aspects of male relations are, in part, explainable in relation to the same features of mining work. Competitiveness and antagonism are related to that aspect of the mining process which facilitates the placing a premium on maximum productivity in masculine identity. They are also related to the ever present potential of death in the pit. Antagonism is, as I argue later, a form of continual testing of the resilience of relations. The principles and mores are in part explainable as a consequence of the cooperation necessitated by the mining process. Co-operation was essential, especially in teams, but also between individual hewers and datal workers, to the pursuit of maximum productivity. Co-operation and mutual responsibility was essential to the minimization of this potential danger; it should be clear that the reckless pursuit of productivity (i.e. productivity without due regard to time consuming safety procedures) endangered the lives of others working on the seam.

This type of technical explanation of the principles and mores of male relations, emphasizing the necessity of co-operation, was echoed by a number of the people I worked with.

"*Ya hed t' lorn t' respect and get along even wi' yar worst enemies. Despite aall the differences, wi' wor aall marras when it came doon tuv it....aall in it together.... pit men together, doon that bloody greet black hole. Aye, there waz a comarardary. It's typical o' mining men any place ya gan. It comes doon t' the trust wi' aall hed....and the responsibility. Ee mek a mistake.... gan at it bit fast coz the wife's tappin' ya for mare money or whatever an it's not ownly yarsell that pays the price.*"

(ii) The association of the pit and death: (6) The embellishment of this man's words with an imagery which draws upon a theme of an inextricable association of the pit and death suggests more than the ostensible explanation of the nature of male relations as a consequence of the necessity of safety. This theme pervades all levels of culture in the area. This is evidenced in the common descriptions of the aesthetics of the pit; its morbid darkness, the similarity between the confined space of the face tunnel and a tomb, etc. The association is reflected in the very language of the area. The pitmatic term for the word death is, to have *'ya chocks draan'*. The chocks are draan, or, in other words, the pit props are removed, in order to collapse and terminate the productive life of the seam. The term for burial draws a parallel with entry to the pit face; *'the last-doon bye'* or *'the last-in bye'*. An ever present consciousness of the pit as the site of the burial of men killed in pit accidents was confirmed by one man I spoke to.

"*Fowty five yors in the pit and thorty o' them workin' on the face an' Aa still nivver got ower the fear. Aa wazn't see scared o' gettin' killed. Aa always thowt Aa'd prefor that t' bein' a borden on me family. Besides Aa'm a religious man. Naa, wat use t' get tuv us waz the noises. It's just the coal talkin', tellin' it's fettle. But they're such earie soonds. Divvent get us wrang. Aa'm not superstitious or nout, but wey ya cannat help but think of aall them fellas whose bodies are rested undergroond alongside ya.*"

The imagery of death in the pit also pervades popular poetry and song.

'In gateway number one,

Waz a beggar of a torn,
Each tub to maa despair got off the way,
Me back was scratched and torn,
Wi' liftin' full'ns on,
Huw Aa langed for lowse to bring an end to the day.
But at neet when Aa reposed,
And sleep me eyelids closed,
Aa dreamt aboot that torn, aall through the neet,
It rose before me eyes
Black death in nee disguise,
Aa was glad agyen when mornin' browt the leet.
But this day Aa went in-bye,
The syem sad luk i' me eye,
And got the shock o' me life, for standin' there,
Was an angel - not a divil -Wi' axe and saaw, and a shovel,
And the Lord t' announce, 'ya hewin' days's nee mare'.
From 'The Putter-Lad', (author not known).

(iii) Miner's taboos and their use: The association of the pit and death is also reflected in the practices and taboos which surround mining. A variety of practices were adhered to for fear that failure to do so would be tantamount to inviting pit accidents and death. Miners touched brass objects before going to work, and insisted that fire tongs should be hung upside down. On 'kyebbling' day, the day of the cavel lottery, some men put their cat inside a comfortably warm oven with milk and food, until they returned home after discovering the result of the draw. The most taboo of all objects is the pig. Miners refrained from uttering its name, referring to it instead as, 'P.I.G.', 'Grunter', 'Gissy', 'The Article', or 'roond fat thing wi' stumpy legs'.

It should be pointed out in this context that the suggestion that the outlook of the miner with respect to the risks involved in the job is one of fatalism (see, for example, Williamson (1982:118)) is incorrect. It is true, as pointed out earlier, that most men felt that excessive caution in terms of the adherence to normal safety procedures was no guarantee against accident or death. However, the adherence to these practices (i.e. the touching of brass objects, etc.) suggests that attitudes cannot be characterized as fatalistic, but rather as displaying a sense that protection is a matter beyond practices explainable and understandable in terms of conventional rationality.

It is difficult, given the sparsity of information forwarded to me, to comment on the meanings of such practices and taboos. Attempts to probe for information were usually met with the blind answer that they are just silly superstitions. However, comments made about the pig offer a way into a cautious preliminary explanation.

I cannot rule out the possibility that characterizations of the pig draw on notions from a wider social context and a scope of referents beyond mining. One man suggested to me that miners had adopted ideas about the pig from local fishing people. There are a number of arguments concerning symbolism surrounding the pig and its position in systems of animal classification (see for example, Douglas'(1986) discussion of the pig as anomalous for the Israelites as a cloven hooved carnivore, and arguments covering eating prohibitions concerning animals, which according to the specific culture stem from the fact that they symbolize tabooed incestuous relationships, because of their semi-domestic status. See, for example, Tambiah (1973), Leach (1972), and, more specifically, in relation to the Harris (1980)), any of which may be of significance.

However, it is clear that the mining people attribute their own specific meanings to the significance of the pig. There is a clear concern with pollution. The most important point to make is that there is a clear symbolic distinction between coal and other kinds of dirt. The term dirt, or 'dart' refers, reflecting common English usage, to all dirt, including coal dust. However, different names are given to coal dust and other kinds of dirt. A local poem exemplifies the linguistic and symbolic distinction.

'There's sum folk wad say that Aa'm dorty,
For me tyble's the back o' me shul,
But coal dust's not dorty like muck is,
Aall pitmen, for heartborn cook coal.'
From 'Jack the Coal Man' (Coombs. — —:8).

Whilst coal dust, or 'duff', is both clean and imbued with medically efficacious qualities (another symbolic quality of coal), other kinds of dirt, i.e. 'muck', or 'clarts' (wet muck), are seen as unclean, polluting, and potentially dangerous. This symbolic distinction is implicit in the alternative status criteria and hierarchies in mining employment. The elevated position of the 'stone man' above ordinary miners is, in part, explained by his inhalation of what are perceived to be more dangerous substances than coal dust.

It is the fact that the pig can ingest such polluting substances which make it of significance. However, it is not polluting in itself. If it were so one would expect this to be reflected in dietary prohibitions. The fact that the people of Ashington may not be said to constitute a distinctly separate ethnic or cultural group does not rule out the possibility of maintaining what can be described as dietary prohibitions or at least distinct ideas about the uncleanliness of different kinds of food which are not held by the wider society; for example, no Ashingtonian that I have ever met would consider the idea of eating the most disgusting of fish, the mackerel. Again this is so because it is seen to thrive, as an inshore fish which swims near to where human effluent is disposed, on ordinary dirt, or 'muck' and 'clarts'. It should be pointed out in this context that, indeed, the very value of my argument is that it shows, in contrast to other studies which have focussed on ethnic groups, that systems of animal classification may be linked to occupational groups.

Far from being unclean the pig's meat and blood are pure, edible and efficacious. As one man told me, "*A bucket o' gissy blood on ya leaks works wonders. It's like rocket fuel.*" Another man told me that the grunter is an amazing animal. It eats nothing but, *"rubbish, muck, an' shite, but when ya cut it oppen it's as clean as a whistle."*

It is this ability of the pig to ingest and positively thrive on 'muck', or unclean, polluting, and dangerous dirt, which makes it significant. In its ability to do this it is the converse of the miner whose life is threatened by such substances. This leads to its association with death. One man told me, in his amazement at the characteristics of the pig that it can see into the future; it always turns its arse to an impending storm, well before its arrival. In other words, I would suggest, it is able to foresee 'ill wind'. It is a harbinger of death (7).

A number of men told me that the power of this taboo enabled its effective use. One man relayed the story about a man who was suspected of stealing money from the locker rooms at Ashington pit. The victims of the crime decided to take action. They arranged for a group of men who were just coming off their shift to steal his bait box whilst he was changing into his pit clothes in preparation for the beginning of his own shift. They took the box and quickly drew the head of a 'grunter' on it, and replaced it in his bag. On taking the bait box from his bag he saw the picture, changed back into his normal clothes, and quickly left the pit. His loss of a day's earnings taught him not to steal again. Another man told me that the taboo was utilised similarly in an event during the 1926 strike. The men at the Newbiggin pit were weakening and beginning to drift back to work. In response, a group of men broke into the colliery there and nailed up the decapitated head of a 'grunter' at the entrance to the main shaft. Before the management had time to remove it, some of the miners on their way to the coal face saw the head and refused to go to work. Word of this spread throughout the village and the strike remained firm for a while longer.

(iv) Association through a common suspension between death and life: A number of other related points should be made in addition to the inextricable association between the pit and death. Firstly, it suggests that the act of entering the pit is much more than to enter an arena of danger and potential death. This is explicitly stated in the characterization of pit work as being alongside the souls of the dead. Similarly, the poem, 'The Putter-Lad', emphasises a transition from the drudgery of life to the state of death, but what is interesting is that in reference to the context of the pit, which is its focus, it makes little clear point of demarcation between these states or moments, as though there were no clear distinction. Moreover, the term for burial is as though each previous entry into the pit, had in themselves been previous burials. Secondly, one implication of the taboos is that the avoidance of death is seen to be beyond adherence to safety procedures, conventions of social conduct, or some other such means amenable to explanation at the level of conventional material rationale.

I don't want to deny the kind of technical argument outlined earlier, which characterizes the principles and mores of male relations as, ultimately, a consequence of the exigencies of safety in the pit (however their is a sense, I suspect, that such arguments are the conventional rationalizations of their own symbolism and abstract notions). But, the cultural representation of the miner suggests more than this. Death can be guarded against by a number of means, including the establishment of cooperative relations and mutual responsibility amongst miners, but, protection by such means can never be total. Death is an inherent and unpredictable possibility. Perhaps as a consequence of this the miner is represented as symbolically close to death itself. What I want to suggest is that the miners are represented as apart from normal life and its inherent divisions in a state where they are equal and united by their common condition of a suspension between life and death.

WOMEN

(i) Overt reference to the relationship between the prevention of mining death and the sexual division of labour: Besides natural causes, human error is cited as the main reason explaining pit accidents. The main causes of human error are seen to be the reckless pursuit of productivity, and the miner being in a bad psychological and/or physical condition, or 'fettle'. At one level this gives force to the legitimacy of male forms of leisure. They are represented as a necessary compensation to the hardships of mining. This legitimacy is personified in the characterization of beer as possessing therapeutic qualities; it swills both 'worries' and 'duff' from the body.

> 'Then the buzzer blaas, and man to man, They queue infront o' the cage, For ten lang ooers belaa they'll gan To mek a livin wage. Then who wad dare the man to judge If Sat'day neet he boozes? Aye who amang ye wad begrudge That comfort, if he chooses?'
> From, 'The Foreshift' (Coombs: – – .29)

What is most important to emphasize here is that, along with other agents (deputies, management, etc.), miner's wives are represented as being potentially responsible for mining deaths and their prevention. In the quote outlined earlier which explained male comradeship, a tacit link is made between men's reckless pursuit of productivity and pressure from the wife for added household income (8). Similarly, an alternative explanation of the Woodhorn disaster, which, it is sometimes claimed, was caused by a man carelessly taking a naked light into a gas filled seam, argues that he didn't have his mind properly on the job because he and his wife had been constantly rowing.

(ii) Women, Death, and The Pit - Symbolic Associations: I have stated that the pit is attributed human qualities. It is often, moreover, represented as gendered. The following local poem characterizes the pit as female.

> 'I bide in the darkness,
> With the silence of the grave,

> *Men may pray or beat me,*
> *Yet never see me wave.*
> *With boys toiling tortured,*
> *And sweating till they're tired,*
> *There above bright world you wait me,*
> *I'll always be required.*
> *I lie below without a voice,*
> *No body, heart or soul,*
> *So mortals bend on your knee,*
> *For I am Black Queen Coal.'*

'Black Queen Coal', (author not known).

The association of a symbolically 'female' pit with death which this poem implies is unquestionably made in the name given by some men I spoke to to the terrifying noise of the settling slate seam roofs; 'The Ashington Banshee' (a female spirit whose wail portends death). Lastly, the practice of keeping a, 'dirty working bed', is significant in this respect. Some miners who refrained from washing their backs kept a separate bed for their own use throughout the working week. This served an obvious practical purpose. However, it is, undoubtedly, a practice of the form outlined before, i.e. one adhered to for fear that failure to do so would be tantamount to inviting pit accidents and death. A number of people I worked with tacitly stated that the practice emphasizes a necessity of sexual abstinence. I suggested that its logic was that, as sex is physically draining, it hinders productive potential and, more importantly, the miner's vigilance. However, this was rejected, though without the offer of alternatives. The practice can only be explained in terms of a hidden logic, which is, I would argue, an association of female sexuality and death (9).

(iii) Conclusions - Mining Death, the Sexual Division of Labour, and Controlling Stereotypes and Taboos: The representation of women as possessing the potential to cause mining death, through the poor execution of their domestic tasks, failing to maintain harmony in the home, bringing unreasonable financial demands through poor budgeting, etc., underlies the symbolic association of women and death. The prevention of death itself is, I would suggest, the imperative legitimising, the rigid sexual division of labour (i.e. in this case, as part of the supportive domestic role, women must maintain financial stability in the home and the psychological and physical condition of the man to prevent error through the over-zealous pursuit of productivity or through ill preparation to do the job), and the constraint of women (i.e. in this case constraint from making financial demands and complaints).

This symbolic association and this moral imperative serve to strengthen the controlling quality of the forms of stereotype outlined (i.e. in this case the representation of women as money grabbing and nagging as a control on their financial or other demands) and give them a greater underlying force. Given this, the use of terms to describe the nagging wife, in the poem presented before, such as and 'bury', may, perhaps, not be regarded as coincidental.

Some of these points are encapsulated in a taboo which is held as widely as that concerning the pig. It is considered unlucky and dangerous to see any woman whilst on the way from the home to the 'back shift'. At one level the taboo serves to control potential sexual liaison outside marriage. More importantly, it represents the domestic domain as the appropriate sphere within which women should operate. Its emphasis on their confinement to this domain, enforced by the threat of death if transgressed, symbolizes the imperative of women's necessary uncritical devotion to their supportive role within this context. Fundamentally, it reinforces the symbolic representation of women as potential bringers of death if out of place.

'REAL COMMUNITY'

> *'Better than aall is the closeness of friends,*
> *Aroond us that help us to bear,*
> *The many discomforts that poverty sends,*
> *For of these nearly aall have their share.*
> *There are also the gud things in life, be it said,*
> *Forbye it's mare unpleasant labours,*
> *Consarn for your welfare, material aid,*
> *Are riches enjoyed b' gud neighbours'.*
> From 'The Raa', (author not known).

The term generally referred to in the characterization

of native community is 'real community', or it is described as being characterized by 'real community spirit'. The terms implicitly refer to what can be called communal sociability and co-operation. Reference to mining and the north-south relation are central to the explanation of these qualities in the ways outlined. However, additionally, representations of these qualities convey an underlying picture of the way in which community and a vaguely defined set of agencies of power such as the state are related. In addition to the exploitative aspect of this relation, community is also represented as autonomous of, and, to an extent, politically opposed to, these agencies.

Communal Sociability and Co-operation

The central celebrated manifestation of this quality of communal sociability is the open-door policy of the colliery home. Humorous accounts which follow a similar story line are a constant source of nostalgic amusement. The husband comes back from a hard day's work to an empty home where he is surprised to find new wallpaper. He thinks nothing of it and puts it down to his wife's constant reshaping of the home. So, he puts his feet up to rest, but Mrs Jones from next door enters in her underwear, and in a state of embarrassment and shock, exclaims, "Aa wad hev put me best bloomers on if Aa'd knaan you were callin'", etc. People stated that the back door was always left open, partially to emphasize the lack of crime in the community, but also, more importantly, to emphasize that neighbours could walk freely into each other's homes, as if reflecting a communal as opposed to privatized existence.

Secondly, the people I worked with interpreted the practice of New Year's Eve 'First-Footing' as the most important celebration of this quality of communal sociability. I witnessed the practice as still in existence. People stock their living rooms with snacks and drinks, and invite callers, many of whom are total strangers, to toast in the new year with them. This is not a practice which is confined to the area, but, in this context, it has a special added dimension. The caller must knock on the door with a piece of coal which is then thrown into the fireplace of the host. At one level the act is seen to celebrate an intention of communal sociability, expressed in the act of freely entering and leaving people's homes, and partaking of their refreshments, and in gift giving of one's own coal to light others' fires. But, at another level, the centrality of coal in the practice expresses the fact that this communal sociability is based on a perceived common dependence on coal.

The central celebrated manifestation of the co-operative aspect of community is the system of roles and obligations beyond the household which were at least evident in times of crisis, and which, undoubtedly, compensated for the inadequacies of the area's infrastructure. For example, neighbours were expected to help with the laying-out of the dead and provide a wailing service, or when people fell sick or were injured, neighbours were expected to help out with domestic chores, making food, sitting children, etc. Neighbours were also expected to help out financially in certain circumstances; organizing collections, providing loans, or paying the less affluent, such as widows, to do tasks they themselves could perform. People became informal unpaid specialists in these respects, and became inseparably identified with these roles; Annie the wailer, Bessie the midwife, Bessie the spoon (the abortionist), etc. As pointed out earlier, these roles were essentially held by women.

At a fundamental level the characterization of the area as consisting of 'real communities' is critically juxtaposed to the south which is seen to consist of atomistic settlements. Additionally, perceptions of the north-south relation and the life seen to be characteristic of mining communities inform explanations of the genesis of this 'real community.' Accounts of the history of the area stress hardship. All aspects of the mining existence personify this hardship (poverty, drudgery, death, crippling illness, etc.), but this hardship is also largely attributed to regional political favouritism and the exploitation of the area. Communal sociability and co-operation are seen as responses to, and, as the poem above expresses, compensations for the hardship.

Autonomy and Political Opposition

One important manifestation of the conceptualization of the north as the victim of exploitation, and regional political favouritism, is a critical regard for official agencies of provision, with the following consequences. It is this very distrust which fuels a belief that the individual is ultimately responsible for his/her welfare, a point I explore later. The representation of local communities as essentially co-operative entities is explicitly related to this. The community is seen and celebrated as a more efficient source of care and welfare provision, as I demonstrate later in discussion of the symbolic reconstitution of community roles in the context of the clubs for the elderly. Similarly, a number of people I spoke to regarded specific social contexts such as the working men's clubs as more appropriate and superior centres of information on a range of subjects, even those concerning officialdom, than the appropriate official sources. In this sense the perceived cooperative quality of community is represented as an expression of community autonomy. In the discussions in the clubs for the elderly much is made of the historical examples of such autonomy; for example, the co-operative society and co-operative stores, the working men's clubs, etc., i.e. the alternative infrastructure.

The representation of community as autonomous is complemented by its representation as the affective basis of political power in the industrial and political struggles which have marked the area's history. The people I worked with emphasized that it was the co-operative quality of the community which enabled survival through long periods of strike action. Moreover, the community is perceived as the agency which enforced militant solidarity.

THE CENTRALITY OF MINING TO COMMUNITY IDENTITY, AND THE INVERSION OF PUTATIVE IMAGES

This sub-section emphasizes the utmost centrality of mining to community identity. At the most fundamental level it pervades the very language of the area. Secondly, it is the case that when one thinks of Ashington one thinks of coal; coal is the substance with which the area is inextricably identified, both externally, and internally. It stands for the totality of perceived features of the area, and its relationship to the world beyond its boundaries. The imagined view of the outsider, or the putative view, is predominantly negative. This is, perhaps inevitable when coal, a substance commonly characterized as mere dirt outside the mining community, is central to identity. But, in the social contexts in which I worked, these putative views are redressed, and this process is prefaced at a symbolic level by a reinterpretation of the meaning of coal which strips it of many of its negative connotations.

Accent and Language

Accent and language are a central focus in the celebration of demarcation between north and south. The mere mention of specific words, or the exaggerated presentation of local accent with an exaggerated simultaneous translation are unending sources of hilarity. The humour stems from the rightly perceived imponderability to outsiders of what is at the same time a variation of English. An extract from a piece read out for the amusement of the members at the Oakville centre exemplifies this. A small girl tells of her Sunday afternoon outing.

'*Eftor wad-wat-ea mean' wor Jean went up t' thon farm abeun the pit heaps wi wor tyke.*' 'After we had had our tea my sister Jean and myself went to the farm beyond the pit heaps. We took our dog with us.'

'*Wi' played hitchy-dabber an' on the way wi' stopped off t' hoy a few clinkers and roondies at the spuggies an' linties.*'

'We played hop-scotch, and on the way we stopped off to throw a few large cinders of bastard coal and larger pieces of pure coal at the sparrows and linnets.' 'Wor Jean sez,

"*Aa'll race ya doon hinnie.*'

'My sister Jean then challenged me to a race.'

'*Wey, wi' wor lowpin' doon, but shi' dunched us.*'

'As we were leaping our way down, unfortunately,

she bumped into me'.

'*Aa cowped me creels an' went stottin' doon an' landed square on me dowps.*'

'I turned a somersault and bounced all the way to the bottom, where I landed on my backside.'

'*Aa tell ya man, Aa cald the donart a few names.*'

'I firmly rebuked the silly girl'.

Exaggerated differences in language in the context of the north-south juxtapositional relation (for example, reflecting political aspects of the relation, working class to posh), play a part in the representation and celebration of community, but the particular language and accent that is celebrated is, of course, the one which is specific to this small area, i.e. not to the north or even to the north east, whose cluster of accents is referred to as 'Geordie', but to this small cluster of mining villages. It is referred to as the 'Ashington Pitmatic'. It has three important features. It is grounded in 'Border Northumbrian'; the variety of the English language which is seen to characterize the area of mid-Northumberland to the border with Scotland. However, as Chaplin argues, the dialect was modified by the influx of miners from other areas, who, nevertheless, assimilated Northumberland speech (in Reed.1975:1). Chaplin goes on colourfully to describe the resultant dialect as a 'polyglottal buzz'. The third major feature is the 'Pitmatic'. Graham states in definition of this, that, "the northern coal miners had certain words and expressions peculiar to themselves." (1980:36). It is more than this; not a fixed dialect, but an ongoing linguistic process whose form is entirely different between mining communities. The 'pitmatic' refers, I would suggest, to this process, where pit terminology is taken and generated into nouns, verbs, adjectives, adverbs, phrases, and so on, which are developed for metaphorical usage in everyday reality, as the following examples demonstrate.

(i) 'Cowps hor creels'-Turns a somersault. The wordcowp, which means, in this context, to turn. Creels are baskets. Such creels were once used in low seams to collect the coal. To cowp the creel meant to turn the basket to empty the coal once it had been dragged out from the seam.

(ii) To 'Heedgehog'- To criticize or intentionally cause someone problems. A heedgehog is a section of conveyor belt cable which has frayed and developed into a ball of spikes like a hedgehog. When moving, it can be extremely dangerous and is a common source of injury or death.

It should be noted that by its nature the 'Pitmatic' is a form more developed and practiced amongst men, such that when women told me that they couldn't understand what the men were on about, they were not merely referring to the specificity of male subject matter, i.e. to the difficulty of understanding shop talk, but also to a problem of language. Cultural differences between men and women are, then, compounded at a fundamental linguistic level. (10).

The Inversion of Putative Images

Despite the fact that accent is a central focus for celebration of identity it is also perceived as both fuelling and forming a part of a host of negative northern stereotypes of which the people I worked with are acutely, and perhaps exaggeratedly, aware. They were keen to redress these and the image of the north propagated by a diet of idealized T.V. dramas (for example, 'When the boat comes in') and documentaries focussing on the north's many social problems. Examples of perceived stereotypical oppositions of southerner-northerner are, complexity-simplicity, intelligence-ignorance, and cultured-coarse.

The negative identity is two-fold in the case of Ashington. Its local identity is as the black mark on Northumberland's green and pleasant land. Its nicknames are invariably negative: for example, 'The Windy City' (referring to the cold wind that blows directly up Ashington's main street because of its perfect positioning in direct opposition to the north sea). At my school in Morpeth the girls and boys who were sent in from Ashington for showing academic potential thought unusual in the area were referred to by the more vicious and racist amongst us with a double entendre; 'The Black Scum'. Local historians, preoccupied with the rural splendours of Northumberland and a romantic feudal past, make their point by simply omitting reference to both Ashington and the mining industry, (for example, Leach(1986)). The dominant image is, however, of Ashington as a dirty town; polluted by the smog and besmirched by the black dust of the mining industry. As Chaplin states, in commenting on the relative newness of Ashington as a town, 'where Morpeth stems from antiquity, Ashington is red raw beneath it's grime' (in Reed.1975:1). The people I worked with take this on board in self identification. However, the reflectively used term, 'us dorty folk' is instantly understood as referring to more than an awareness of an image of uncleanliness. It expresses the totality of such perceived negative images. The dirt referred to is the coal, oils, and fumes generated in the mining process which, thus symbolically demarcates these people. This differentiation is bluntly drawn in local popular culture:

'His pit claes has that special tang,
Of coal, and grease, and smoke,
That to colliery hooses aall belang,
And singles oot pit folk.'
From,'The Foreshift' (Coombs:— —.27)

Whilst accent and an image of uncleanliness are themselves recognised as aspects of a general demeaning image of this area and the north generally, their celebration is indicative of the fact that such demeaning images are not redressed through their rejection. The same applies to other aspects of the negative differentiation of northerner and southerner. This fact is recognised by local media and advertising. One advertisement gave particular pleasure to the people I worked with when it was first shown on television because of its treatment of this aspect of a north-south divide.

Young William is sent on his first mission by his employers, Scottish and Newcastle Breweries, to market a new make of beer in the south of England. In each pub he visits the landlord tastes the beer, spits it out in disgust, and throws young William out onto the street. After considerable effort the young salesman returns to Newcastle, disheartened. Not even the welcoming sight of the Tyne bridge can cheer him up. Fearing for his job he timidly reports to the director to give his progress report. After telling his woeful tale the director congratulates him, offers him instant promotion, and promptly phones his colleagues to tell them the news about their new product; 'it's a success!'

The advertisement makes the point that southern disapproval is the ultimate indication of quality. The humour stems from its drawing upon a culture which systematically takes the negative stereotypical images of the north which are perceived to be held in the south, explains them as misunderstood, and the misunderstanding to be indicative of ignorance or some other such negative facet, reinterprets them, and explains the features of the area upon which they are based as manifestations of positive as opposed to negative qualities. For example, the men I socialised with in the working men's club were keenly aware of the image of the beer swilling northern man, but reinterpreted their actions as a manifestation of a northern communal sociability, which cannot be fully appreciated by a southerner, living his/her privatised existence in his/her, atomistic settlement. The function of beer is encapsulated in its name; 'Discourse Oil'.

This form of inversion is mirrored at a fundamental level in the treatment of the stuff which symbolically expresses differentiation. Recognition of the harmful, polluting properties of coal (the cause of lung disease, blood poisoning, and physical scarring) is accompanied by its representation, at a conscious level, and, more powerfully, at a symbolic level, as possessing efficacious qualities.

Thus, to summarize, the totality of perceived negative images of the people of the area are encapsulated in an image of uncleanliness, i.e. 'the dorty folk'. The root of this is identification with coal and mining. A process of reinterpretation of the perceived negative images is mirrored at a fundamental level in the reinterpretation of coal as a curative and thus, ultimately, pure substance, such that the identity the 'dorty folk' is in fact a positive one.

CONCLUDING COMMENTS

I will elucidate one or two key, and other impressionistic, points which are implicit throughout this section. I will refer to an emotive letter written to one of the local newspapers. The letter was written in reply to a previous letter which had suggested that the imminent closure of Ashington colliery would herald the beginning of a bright new era in the future of the area.

In reply to "The beginning of a better age".

Yes David Hides we know the benefits of pit closure here in Newbiggin. Men have been freed from the toil that they sweated blood for a miserly wage, to take up clean and safe work in the factories of Cramlington. The pit blighted our landscape and polluted our environment. Now you can breathe without your lung-box swelling, and the awful sulphuric stinks of rotten eggs and onions have gone. The trucks thunder down the high street no more, risking life and limb of all those who stepped near. Gone are the stinking pit pools that our bairns would come back from clarted up to the eyeballs. We can paint our doors and windows knowing that within days they won't be tarnished. Best of all, our women can hang their clean white clothes out on the line without fear that with a sudden change in the wind they'll be black again within minutes.

But for all the clean air and grassy mounds that were the stinking slag heaps, is Newbiggin a better place? Few would answer yes. Where are the characters now? As for neighbours, well I wouldn't know mine from Adam. It's not long since I passed pleasantries to the man next door under the door of the intimate confines of the 'nettie'. And they wouldn't begrudge you a helping hand. These were the things which made this place special and they disappeared with the grime.

You see Mr Hides, that very grime stands for everything that we stand for. Our history, our independence, our battles for a better life, and above all, our community. It is the mark of a rare breed which without its mark is losing its pedigree. So if there were a choice between the clean air that we all love, and the grime, I know where I would put my tick. In his poem 'The Pit Heap' our own poet Fred Reed expresses my sentiments perfectly.

'Aa knaa the blot hes gyen at last,
Green fields cum inta view,
Strange silence broods where once the blast, Of despot buzzers blew.
But if them wheels could torn agyen,
Wor joy ne tungue could tell.
We'd put up wi' the blot and stain
And dust and reek and smell.'

Mr Hides, I think you will understand my message, so don't be rash. The loss of Ashington colliery should be mourned and not celebrated. You are losing much, much more than a handful of jobs,

Yours faithfully,

J. Blades. Newbiggin.

(Source not known – article circulated in clubs).

At one level the letter is a romantic reminiscence of how life used to be. However, more importantly, it ramifies the centrality of mining to the community. Coal is explicitly used to symbolize the totality of social features which are seen to be specific to this area. The words describing coal as, 'the mark of a rare breed which without its mark is losing its pedigree', suggests that not only does it symbolize these internal features, but that it is, in a sense, a sign, to the world outside its boundaries, of its cultural purity (11). However, additionally, in drawing the analogy between cultural purity and coal, it expresses the reality of the culture of the area's total dependence on the mining industry. This was clearly stressed in the miners' strike of 1984-5 which was portrayed by the N.U.M. as, 'a last, and in the event unsuccessful, attempt by a sector of the traditional working class to defend their jobs and their communities' (Cole, 1989:24). This raises two important points. First, given this dependence, the representation and celebration of community as being characterized by autonomy and political opposition must be read as an inverted expression of reality, i.e. the area has always been dependent on the fluctuations of an external market, the ideological whims and energy policies of government, and, prior to nationalization, the changing employment, pay, and investment policies of the private coal companies. As a consequence, the area has been totally dependent on the world beyond its boundaries. This has not changed (especially given the number of people relying on state benefits). Secondly, given this dependence, and given the fact that the struggle to keep Ashington colliery was inevitably lost, leaving only one non-private mine in the area in operation, the question must be raised of how a picture of community which is so dependent on mining as its referent can be sustained. The people I worked with unquestionably described their community as a mining community, when in fact there is almost no mining industry to justify. This apparent contradiction will form a major strand of the following section.

2-CHANGE AND THE RECONSTITUTION OF AN IDEALIZED COMMUNITY

MORAL AND SOCIAL DECLINE: THE EROSION OF COMMUNITY

Despite the fact that I have outlined a series of features which are represented and celebrated as characteristic of local community, and have shown that the major referent for this, the mining industry, has largely disappeared, the people I worked with do not engage in an act of self deception. Debate and local popular culture, which is used in celebration and generated in the clubs for the elderly, directly addresses the issue of change. These features of community are the central concerns. A coherent body of ideas is clearly evident. These ideas emphasize a social and moral decline which is, in part manifested and rooted in a perceived breakdown of the type of community which they celebrate. It is this body of ideas which I will address here by a summary of its main features, and with supporting ethnographic data and interpretation.

The breakdown of family structure

(i) Order-Chaos:
Hilda: "*The times waz always tight in wor day. Wi' hed t' mek dee wi' wat the men orned. Nee mare an' nee less mind. And mind wi' managed. Sometimes Aa wonder how, but wi used wor inginuity and were careful. Ya couldn't say that for the young'ns noowadays. Haf o' them's oot at the bingo while the' hoose is fallin' apart coz the' hevn't payed the bills.*"

Whilst the hardship of the past bred the need for financial prudence and efficient management within the home, rising incomes and the availability of credit have reduced the need for self sufficiency, financial and domestic managerial skills have disappeared, and the young have learned to become irresponsible with their money. The result is domestic chaos. The image portrayed is encapsulated in a term used to describe the young, 'The Bingo Generation'. Its meaning is conveyed in a popular poem recited in some of the clubs.

'*Ha! Bingo! Bingo! It's a word for me Like Ali Baba's oppen sesame, And one-time cinemas noo howld delights And witchin' spells like them Arabian Nights, With Kelly's eye and Hoose and legs elivvin Fair music soondin' in a blue-smoke hivvin, And Aa'll howld up me bingo card some day And knaa at last a trissure's com' me way. Back hyem the fire should be* oot, Aa think. And aall them dorty dishes in the sink! Me bairns, locked oot, are plain' in the streets, And cowpin' bins and hoyin' styens at leits. Aa knaa some foalks'll blare, "Ee, whaat a shem!" But Aa've a reit t° plissures syem as them. Whaat? Drama? Byuks? Good music? Poetry? Ye Gimmor! What's this poor world comin' tee?"

'Bingo' (Reed.1977:23).

(ii) The strength of marriage-the weakness of marriage:

Barbara: "*The problem wi' the young folk is they've nee respect for marriage. Forst problem comes along an' theyor oot. Nivver mind the bairns....theyor oot. Wey, in wor day ya hed nee choice. Ya Just stuck it oot. Nee tee ways."*

"*Wi aall hed wor problems. Aa mind many a time runnin' t' me motha. Shi Just telt us t' strettin' it oot.... the rows an' such like ya knaa. Aa stuck it oot an' it's worth it. Aa've got three fine bairns oot've it. Nivver a knock on the door for one of them. Aye wor generation hed t' stick it oot in them days.*"

The family used to be rigid and unbreakable. Marriage was not entered into lightly, as one knew that it was a commitment for life. Nowadays there are increasing numbers of one parent, and broken families. Young people enter marriage lightly, and when they realize this involves making sacrifices they can't take to, they refuse to compromise and, instead, choose divorce.

(iii) Sexual morality-sexual immorality:

Hilda: "*Marriages is different noowadays. It's aall aboot sex. The' get bored soon an' gan off wi' theyor fancy men. It usually ends up in the divorce courts. Ya see we Just didn't think aboot that. Aa married my man because Aa loved him,* and mind Aa med sure ee waz respectable enough for me parents."

Doris: "Aye, but ya cannat blame the bairns. It's respectable these days. On the telly it's aall sex, sex, sex."

Hilda: "Ya reit theyor mind."

Doris: "Aye it's disgusting. And Aa mean... hev ya seen that Anne Diamond woman.....on 'Breakfast Time' telly. Aa divvent knaa how the' allow hor on the telly. Aa mean..five months pregnant an' nee husband into the bargain. You've got to laugh mind. Aa'm haf expecting hor t' hoy up wi' mornin' sickness."

One reason for the breakdown in the strength of the family unit is the liberal climate surrounding sexual morality. Sex out of wedlock is considered legitimate nowadays. The media plays a part in this legitimation by screening programmes with a sexual content and allowing deviants in the context of an ideal family structure, such as single parent mothers, to hold important positions of respect. They argue that a promiscuous generation has been produced which builds its relationships on the weak footing of sexual attraction, rather than love and a commitment to maintain a strong family unit for life. In the past, sex out of wedlock was taboo, and relationships were built on a much firmer footing than mere attraction.

(iv)Women: Housewives-Sex objects: It should be clear that at all these levels women are seen to take much of the responsibility.

Doris: "It's nee wonder the bairns is like they are. Aa

blame the women folk. They're ower busy mekin' themselves look beautiful for the' fancy men." According to the ideal family structure outlined earlier, women are responsible for the order of the home and cohesion of the family unit. A perceived breakdown in these respects as, in part, explained by changes in sexual morality, is accompanied by arguments emphasizing the changing identity of women (see Szurek's detailed account of perceived changes in this respect(1985)). An increasing significance of women's sexual identity has involved the deprivation of their traditional supportive role and the loss of its contingent skills, and the loss of commitment to home and family life generally.

Autonomy and independence - dependence

Bart: "*Aa knaa it's bad like....since aall the pits' gone but it gets me when the' tell ya how hard the' gettin' it. The' divvent knaa the meanin' o' the ward. The' pampered man. Aa've come back eftor a bad cavel' afore wi' barely enough t' buy the food. Vat did wi' dee? Wi' med dee....went scavingin' for bits o' coal, an' wi' grew wor own stuff. These young'ns wad-n't hev a clue man. The' cannat stand on theyor own two feet.*"

Younger generations are increasingly less self-sufficient. They have become dependent on state welfare provision, and, moreover have developed a sense of automatic entitlement to support.

The Breakdown of Community

Accounts of the current moral/social climate in the area stress the breakdown of co-operation between neighbours, and communal sociability. Accounts of people's attempts to help neighbours that are met with refusal or little reciprocity are a constant source of conversation. A perception of the breakdown of communal sociability is tacitly expressed in romantic reminiscences about times lost.

Bart: "*It's not Lang since ya cud walk doon North Seaton Road an' knaa nine oot o' ten fyeces. Gan doon noo an' it feels like yar a stranger in yar own toon.*"

People cited two main reasons for this situation. Rising incomes have removed the hardships which in the past created the need for people to help one another. Additionally, the rising incomes of recent years have served to promote materialistic values and material competitiveness. The common phrase, "keeping up wi' the Jones" is applied literally to describe the young. Secondly, there is an awareness of how leisure time is spent less and less in the public sphere. Younger generations are much maligned for their unsociability and lack of inventiveness in the field of leisure. The advent of television and video is seen as a major source of the blame.

"*T. V. for me. Neit eftor neit*
1171.1 eyes fixed on the box
Aa tyek me harmless pleasure though

The whole creation rocks.
Ne reachin' oot,-ne rebels ire,
Ne frenzy t' create.
Aa jist sit on me dowp and bowk
And dimly vegetate."
'The Modern Citizen', (author not known).

The most alarming consequence of all the changes expressed by the people I worked with is a perceived breakdown in law and order. Fuelled by the local press, even the smallest of crimes are a constant source of conversation in the clubs for the elderly, and are portrayed as the evidence of Ashington's demise in this respect. Descriptions of the present emphasizing a state of criminality, and violence in particular, are sharply contrasted with the order and harmony of Ashington's former years. The personification of this order is the celebrated 'open door' practice which, it is claimed, has ceased to exist because of the fear of burglary.

Local referents

(i)Woodbridge: Though generalized to the whole of the Ashington area, accounts of this nature have a primary geographical referent. As the centre for Ashington council's location of 'problem clients' (the homeless, single parent families, those resettled after separation, the long term dependent), the large council estate in the centre of Woodbridge provides an empirical basis upon which an identity for the whole of that area has been constructed. It symbolizes everything that is bad about contemporary Ashington. Some people I spoke to even referred to it as, 'The Midden' (i.e. where Ashington dumps its shit). Its overriding image is that of its violence. Its club, 'The Premier', is the symbolic stage where Ashington's decline is manifested and acted out. When I informed a group of elderly men that I planned to visit the club I was sharply warned off.

Bart: *"Ee must be feelin' depressed Jim."*

Jim : *"Aye, or not reit in the heed."*

Bart: *"Aa think thon pretty lass wi' saw him with must o' givin' him the hoy, an' ee's decided t' tek ees life into ees own hands."*

Andy: *"What are you lot on about now?"*

Bart: *"Wey Aa can think o' plenty nicer ways of endin' it aall than an evenin' doon where your plannin'."*

Andy: *"What do you mean?"*

Bart: *"The forst thing the' should a' telt ya when ya come up here is to avoid that place. It's fuckin' evil. Ya'll likely get dadded afore ya arrive. The' bloody animals doon theyor....always scrappin'. A lad waz bottled theyor not see lang since. And, mind, divvent touch any o' the lasses. The' hev theyor own strains o' the dose doon there."*

(ii)Old-new housing: Having said this, Woodbridge's significance lies not only in that it is seen to represent a concentration of the social problems central to the representation of Ashington's moral and social demise. The fact that it is a modern housing development, built on a site where colliery rows once stood is also of importance. This point can best be illustrated by quoting the comments of, firstly, an elderly man I spoke to who assessed the pros and cons of a move from his home in the Hirst rows to Woodbridge, and secondly another elderly man who was angered by a similar, but more reputable housing development in Ellington.

"Aa can understand wat the' see in it. The amenities is better. They've got better gardens an' wey they're secluded like... divvent get nee distorbance an' such like. Aa cannat say wi' didn't think aboot a change worsells when the' put them up, but when it come tuv it wi' med the right decision. Wey Aa mean that's the problem. They're ower secluded. They've got the shops an' that, but the' hevn't nee spirit. Nee-body talks. This place mightn't be ideal, but Aa knaa me neighbours for better, or worse. Aa hev a bit chatter oot the back there. Aa keep in touch."

"The folks from the raas is movin' ower theyor. They've put the trees up so the' divvent hev t' see us dorty folk. They've soon forgotten where they're fram. Silly folks, tornin' theyor backs like that. They've forgotten wat med them...wat med this place. Them hooses hev tekkin' the heart oot've It."

The ascendancy of modern housing causes offence, whether it be in Woodbridge, Ellington, or any other part of the area, precisely because it represents much more than a material change. Accounts of life in the colliery houses, specific aspects of their usage, and their specific physical features, play a central role in the elderly people's representation of community. According to the descriptions of the colliery home the difference between front and back is apparently that between decorative and functional. To the back of the house is the back yard where household chores such as the drying of clothes and the beating of carpets was done. Beyond the yard on a dirt track are the toilets, wash houses, refuse middens, and trolley lines. To the front of the house there is a small garden which was kept neat and clean, and beyond this a pathway. The front of the house was cleaned copiously and particular attention was paid to the front doorstep which was rubbed regularly with a small clay block called a 'holy stone'. It was the outward sign to passers-by of the order and cleanliness of the interior (see Williamson's development of this point 1982:126).

Front and back doors were used differently. I shall explain these separately at length here. The back door was for normal everyday usage. It was left open, facilitating the easy access of neighbours and visiting local tradespeople. In contradistinction to this the front door was kept locked and normally only used by strangers and members of higher status occupational groups; doctors, colliery management, and so on.

The differential usage of front and back serves, I would argue, in the expression of social phenomena. It symbolizes, the boundaries of community membership (i.e. stranger-local), notions of status differentiation, and, more importantly, the immersion of individual in community. The interpretation and celebration of the open door policy of the colliery home as being an indication of the communal sociability which is central to the notion of community represented in the context of the clubs, reflects this immersion. In different ways other physical features of the rows, which are highlighted in the accounts of the people I worked with, are symbols of this immersion. The communal facilities are central to the characterization of life in the rows as life in the public domain. Women collected to talk in each other's back yards. Men loitered on the corners of the rows, usually in their 'schools'. Children played together outside on the dirt track. Monday was washing day when the women who were served by the same stand tap and wash house came together with equal quantities of coal to work at starting the fire which heated the water, etc.

Another aspect of the individual's immersion is the denial of privacy which is seen to have characterized life in the rows. One woman explained that nobody could keep a secret and nobody pretended to because the proximity of the houses and their thin walls facilitated eavesdropping. A central source of amusement was listening to the next door neighbours' arguments and fights, after which the events were reported to others in the row, and if a particular argument had been caused by some great misdemeanour neighbours would openly give the guilty party a stony faced glare the following morning. Similarly, the instant laughter which any mention of 'the nettie' provokes is no coincidence (see earlier quote from newspaper about conversations under the nettie door). What is normally the most private of acts was public.

Having shown that the family normally used the back door for entry to, and exit from the home, on special occasions the front door was used. Most notably, it was used for the entry of a new baby into the family, if it had been born outside, at weddings, and at funerals. The demarcation between community membership and outside which the differential usage expresses is also important in this context. In the first case the practice symbolizes the entry of the child into the family, and by implication, because of the blurring of public and private within the home, into the community generally. The converse is the case for the deceased in funerary practice. An extended period of mourning for the family concerned, where neighbours did not visit, and the windows were blacked out, represents a exclusion of the family from the community too, albeit temporarily. In the case of marriage the usage symbolizes the departure of the bride or groom from one family unit, and entry into another. As usage of the front door symbolizes exit from, or entry to, the interrelated spheres of both family and community, its usage may be selective, depending upon what is being symbolized. In the former two cases, both family and community are the subjects, whilst in the case of marriage between partners in the community, a transition between families is the sole focus.

Given what I have said, the copious attention given to the front doorstep cannot be regarded as a mere matter of aesthetics and management of putative impressions. The doorstep is a threshold in the fullest sense of the word; between, inside and outside, family and non-family, community and non-community, and, perhaps, between life and death.

It is possible to compare the old and new housing and show in which specific material ways the design features of the former, which played a part in symbolizing aspects of life and death in the ways outlined above, have been removed. In the new housing public and private are rigidly demarcated. This is ensured by the internalization of previously communal facilities, making the area behind and in front of the house mere access ways and byways rather than centres of communal activity, the emphasis on enclosure (i.e. fencing off from the public gaze), and distance between houses (i.e. detachment, and separation by wide roadways). The other significant difference between the old and new housing concerns their points of entry. Whilst the former has two points of entry, the latter has only one; the back door merely being a means of access to the private garden. Whilst in the colliery housing the differential usage could symbolize, for example, notions of status and community membership, in the new housing the means to such symbolism is denied. The one point of public and private entry is a largely meaningless and functional threshold.

My argument is consistent with one central tenet in the accounts of the demise of the area; the breakdown of community as manifested in the decline of communal sociability and cooperation. Whilst the usage and the features of the colliery home symbolize immersion in the community, life in the new housing estates can be represented, given what I have said, as one of alienation from community life. Both points are covertly substantiated. Accounts of the communal sociability of the past are very much dependent on life in the rows for their reference, and the theme of alienation stood out in the descriptions of new housing (see first quote).

The least that can be said is that, as the latter of the quotes presented above emphasizes, the replacement of old housing by new is a material symbol of the destruction of a cherished social order. My account of the symbolic aspects of the colliery home may give another insight into why the colliery home is such a potent symbol for the people I worked with, beyond this consciously celebrated communal sociability. Though I must admit a certain insecurity in presenting an interpretation which goes well beyond the interpretations forwarded to me, I feel that I have teased out an implicit logic; expressed the unsaid.

SELECTIVITY, EXAGGERATION, IDEALIZATION AND CONTRADICTION IN THE REPRESENTATION OF THE PAST AND IMAGES OF CHANGE.

It is not my intention systematically and comprehensively to take to task the representation of community outlined in Part I, and the accounts of change generated in the contexts in question. Aspects of them can be shown to be based on fact, substantiated, added to, or, conversely, criticised. What is clear, however, is that such representations are subject to a considerable degree of selectivity, exaggeration, idealization, and contradiction. I will attempt to elucidate these features of their construction here.

Outmoded morality and efficacies of the modern moral/social order

Alongside the tone of indignation which surrounds the accounts of change, people, in contradistinction, admit to the advantages of changes in the moral/social climate, the disadvantages of the moral/social climates that they have lived through, and the fact that it was the oppressive nature of these, rather than any particular strength on their behalf, which explained their actions. For example, Barbara, the woman whom I quoted complaining about the weakness of marriage, explained that her marriage had been particularly problematic and oppressive, and that, had divorce been a viable and acceptable alternative at the time, she would have opted for it. Doris, whom I quoted complaining about the decline in sexual morality, conceded that the views of many of her generation about sex had been moulded by a moral and religious climate that had perpetuated misinformation,

"*If Aa'd knaan wat Aa fund oot efter Aa waz married Aa*

wad've done a bit more kissin' afore at least."

There is also recognition that changes in the climate of sexual morality had brought benefits. The advantages of living together before marriage are recognized.

Barbara: "Aa must've been stupid. Aa went doon t' stay wi' war John an' ees lass the week afore the weddin'. Ee telt us ee waz hor lodger. Wey Aa, stupid fyeul that Aa am, believed him. Anyway, the' put us in his bedroom. Wey, at least the' telt us it waz his. The'd ruffled the sheets an' that, but there waz nee hairs. Wey Aa realized then the' were mekin' on. Aa cried mesell stupid that night. Ya knaa. It spoilt the magic of it....them hevin' been together in the physical way afore. Aa kept thinkin' o' me fatha. Ee always telt wuz, 'it's alreet for a man t' sow ees seed but not wi' the woman ee loves.' Then Aa thowt, wey the silly owld bugger nivver talked nee sense anyway. An' Aa thowt t' mesell Aa'd rather them live together an' see the' bad sides forst afore discoverin' then later like Aa hed tee."

Similarly, the perceived tendency towards privatism by younger generations in the field of leisure, which on the one hand is represented as a cause of the breakdown of communal sociability is seen to have beneficial consequences. In contradistinction to the image of neglect of the family, Doris explained that,

"Aye, folks is different noowadays. The men divvent gan t' the clubs see much. Folks likes t' stay at hyem....watch telly...spend time in wi' the family like."

Exaggeration and Idealization

It is also clear that representations of the present moral/social climate which inform accounts of change are subject to some considerable exaggeration. To give but one pertinent example, the fears which had been injected into me about the Premier club were sharply dissolved. After plucking up the courage to enter, I walked into a bar which was empty, with the exception two elderly men. The barman explained to me that business was dying fast. Two minor violent events that had occurred some years previously had exacerbated the club's already unjustly bad reputation, and the younger people preferred the new pubs up town anyway.

Whilst assessing the extent of such exaggeration is difficult, this is not the case when considering the portrayal of the past. Alongside the tone of indignation implicit in comparison of past to present, comments, usually made in humour, serve to contradict this picture and show it to be one of considerable idealization.

In characterizing themselves as from a sociable, self-sufficient and inventive generation, in critical contradistinction to the young, they contradict the self image of financial prudence. It is rightly claimed that a plethora of past times which displayed their inventiveness have, or are disappearing, largely because of the advent of television; for example, pigeon racing, wheel coursing (the carcass of a rabbit is pulled along by a bicycle wheel, after which people race their dogs), quoits, cards, pitch and toss (coin flipping competition)(12).

However, the element which binds and generated all these past-times is gambling. As one man told me, *"we'd play anything as long as ya could mek a bob or two on't."* Gambling was not the pursuit of the minority, especially amongst men. One of the privileges of coming of age, which was marked by entry into the pit, was an invitation to join a 'school'; an organized gambling group which met in secluded places to avoid 'cops', i.e. police raids. The name school derives from the fact that the new initiates, who probably had less money anyway, had to serve an apprenticeship, learning how to gamble responsibly, and serving the elders in the group by acting as look-outs.

Despite this emphasis on responsibility, men frequently gambled beyond their means, surviving by borrowing money from the local loan sharks, or selling items from the household. Not only is the ideal of financial prudence questionable, but also, whilst I cannot bring into question the suggestion that the family unit was rigidly structured with a matriarchal head in control of finance, it is clear that the demands of gambling must in many cases have undermined the extent of women's control in this respect. Firstly, the debts accrued by men spending beyond their means needed to be paid off. Secondly, this control was undermined by the practice of 'howldin' back'. It was, I was told, common for hewers' team leaders, who were responsible for distributing wages to the whole team, to consult their workmates about whether they wished their pay slips to be falsely made out such that they could hold back a portion of their income without declaring it to their wives. One man explained to me that his father raised himself from his death bed to collect his final pay packet, rather than having it delivered to the home, so that he could prevent his wife from realizing that he had deceived her about the size of his wages throughout their marriage (13). Finally, it should be stated that, in contradistinction to the image of financial prudence, the much maligned game of bingo is one of the most popular club pastimes.

Similarly, idealization is also evident in comments which contradict the image of a sexually moral past. The same group of women who labelled the younger generations as promiscuous covertly expressed the commonalioty of extra marital sex in former times when they joked about a number of the children in their community, who, though supposedly unrelated, were more than strikingly similar in appearance. The same woman who expressed particularly forthright views suggesting that modern marriages are primarily based on sexual attraction rather than love and commitment, conveyed, through humour, one more reason, if not the overriding one, other than the ones she earnestly forwarded, in the explanation of her decision to marry the man in question.

Hilda: *"Aa went back t' tell me motha a hed a bairn on the way. Shi' called us every name in the book. Aa says, 'divvent blame me, it waz Tommy Burns'* (her future husband) *fault.'"*

Perhaps the most idealized element in the images perpetuated of the past is that of community harmony. A section from a letter in one of the local newspapers accuses the writer of a previous letter of such idealization. The latter had been shocked on returning to the area to confront violence. 'It wasn't like that in the old days!'

"As to the violence you were offered, in our day you wouldn't have been offered, you would have been dadded. There were always short triggered men in Ashington and if you have forgotten that your memory is fading. The Grand Corner at hoying out time was often like the Battle of Hastings, and it was there that the famous battle cry was born "Take no Prisoners." And then on Sunday morning the Salvation Army Band used to plodge through the pools of blood and play hymns. Remember?"

(I.Wilson, Weekly Courier, March 29th 1989:7).

Most of the people I worked with did not deny the existence of violence in the past. However, whilst violence in the present is characterized as a social problem, the violence of yesteryear blends in with the tapestry of descriptions which constitute the idealization of Ashington's past.

Bart: *"Aa remember this place fair hummin'. Sat'day neit the howl world waz oot. Ee young'ns divvent knaa wat ya missin'. It waz great man. Aa knew ivory fyece in ivory club. Am a reit Jim?"*

Jim : *"Wey aye."*

Bart: *"Wi' went roond aall the clubs in the Horst, an' mind come hoyin' oot time aall hell let loose. Wi' had some bashins'. Aa tell ya the' were great times."*

Having said this, distinctions are made between past and present in terms of the type of violence. Violence of the present is usually characterized as indiscriminate. Secondly, distinctions are made in terms of the sub-cultural styles of the perpetrators.

Bart: *"Wi knew who wi' were fightin'. Wi' hed wor enemies, wor rivalries. East Horst boys or whatever. Young'ns noo....mind the' divvent give a shite man. They'll tek it oat on the forst porson the' please. Us lot just hed a good honest scrap....aall consenting. This lot noo it's aall steroids an' pumping iron an' the likes. Aa'll tell ya man some o' them's walkin' fuckin' animals."*

However, what is most surprising is that the basic distinction between past and present (i.e. violence as social problem violence blending into the tapestry of descriptions of an idealized past) holds in the case of violence as a form of collective social sanction, which might be expected to be regarded as legitimate and which is qualitatively similar in present and past. The most prominent example of the treatment of violence in this sense concerned the feelings which were expressed about the recent national strike. Despite some controversy, most people I spoke to considered the strike to have had positive consequences; it had united communities. I arrived after the strike had finished, but whilst I was there the appeal hearings for a number of men convicted of various forms of intimidation were underway. These were a talking point in the clubs for the elderly, and were widely condemned as unnecessary acts of violence in what most had rightly considered to have otherwise been a fairly peaceful campaign. However, as noted before, club members openly and proudly talked of the community enforced solidarity through intimidation of previous strikes, and celebrated the lives of often violent subversive heroes (14).

Similarly, the reality of life in the rows blends into their idealized descriptions. The same features of design which are referred to in descriptions of the communal sociability of the past were the very reasons why their inhabitants and the miners union pressurized for their replacement or modernization. Residents suffered from an array of problems; noise pollution, a lack of the conveniences which modern housing offers, pollution from hundreds of coal burning fires, and insanitary conditions.

The ideal of communal sociability and harmony amongst neighbours is undermined, not only by the humorous accounts of inter-neighbour conflict, which, similarly, blend into this tapestry of the past, but also by the fact that, whilst people emphasize the existence of the open door policy, in reality only certain people, such as close friends, could freely enter. The elderly peoples' interpretation of the practice of 'First-Footing' as a manifestation of communal sociability is, I would suggest, in itself also evidence of idealization in this respect. Its symbolic significance lies in that it occurs between two distinct moments in time. It is in this sense, I would suggest, a liminal moment, outside of time, and, outside of the structure of everyday relations; an antistructural inversion of normally structured, rather than the equal relations, implied in the idea of communal sociability (15).

CONCLUDING COMMENTS:

At one level it is possible to explain the selective representation of past and present, and the consequent contradictions involved in such representation, in terms of incidental features of the lives of the elderly. For example, clearly, since the images of the past are based on memories, the passing of time has facilitated its representation in an idealized form. Secondly, its representation and the representation of the present could be partially a reflection of the location of the elderly in the wider modern social context of Ashington. For example, as I demonstrate later, perceptions of the breakdown of community life may be a consequence of their marginality. In this sense the feelings of living in a strange town or the reservations about moving to Woodbridge (see earlier quote) could be interpreted as the experiencing of, or fear of, social death, perceived as, and explained in terms of social commentary concerning change within the community. Thirdly, there is a sense also in which this selectivity is generated by anger. Many of the people I worked with characterize themselves as a forgotten generation which has been cheated by history. They played a part in the reasons for changes which brought about material and other benefits (for example, their part in the war, their industrial effort, and political and industrial struggle, and the subsequent coming to power of a Labour government, nationalization of the mining industry, the post war economic boom, and so on), but they have seen fewer of the benefits of these changes. Finally, it is clear that the elderly straddle contradictory moral/social climates. There is certainly a sense in which morality moulded in early stages of lives of the elderly maintains an oppressive/ influential force. This is evidenced by the fact that the contradiction of such morality is expressed in humour as if this maintained the ability to shock or embarrass.

However, the representations of change are more than selective. Conversation and celebration in the social arenas of the elderly generate radically polarized representations of past and present, past community and present community, and older and younger generations. Like the southerner and the south, the young and modern day Ashington become the juxtapositional other in the representation of the elderly.

The evidence of this juxtaposition can be pointed to at a number of levels. Woodbridge, in its representation as symbolizing everything that is bad about contemporary Ashington becomes the actual geographical referent in this generational dichotomy. Essential differences between old and young (for example, the characterization of the younger generation as a dependent generation is explained as an inability to stand on their own two feet, rather than in terms of the rise of state support which has facilitated a culture of dependency) are posited. The older generation within this generational dichotomy is idealized at all levels, and even in the expression of contradiction of this ideal. The use of humour in the portrayal of violence, and other such social maladies of their era and generation serves to rid these of the type of 'danger' which is seen to be implicit in the maladies of a similar nature, committed by the young, and of the present. This sanitizing effect of humour then serves to submerge potential contradiction to the ideal.

A number of points should be raised about this process. Firstly, the apparent contradiction pointed to in Part I can be answered. The continued representation of a community whose major referent is the mining industry, alongside an acceptance that, along with the demise of this industry, this community has been fragmented and eroded is not a contradiction. It is clear that the people I worked with are dealing with two distinct notions of community; one of the present, and one 'apparently' of the past. This latter community is essentially 'theirs'. In other words, they are the members of this community, the generational survivors of its era, and the guardians of its values. It is in this sense that I refer to community as 'apparently' of the past, for, I would argue, it is a community which is still existent in the gatherings of the elderly. Its celebration serves in its symbolic reconstitution.

Though this representation of community is by and large based upon the shared experiences of participants, this has its limits. There are significant differences between the elderly. For example, within the clubs there are significant age differences, with consequent differences in incomes and life experiences. However, identification as member of this generation and community is not, I would suggest something which is defined in terms of age cohorts. Rather, it is implicit in ones participation within such arenas. This is, as I show later, borne out by the criticism of peers in the manner that the juxtapositional category of the young is criticized, being suspended within the club contexts, but being aired beyond them. Cross-generational disunity between the elderly in terms of shared experiences was most starkly exemplified in the reception of the forms of entertainment which marked out community as distinct. For many of the club participants the alternative names of local communities and the celebrated features of the colliery home which have been removed through modernization, are unknown. Similarly, in the celebration of identity through the exaggerated presentation of local dialect, the accompanying simultaneous translation does not only serve to intensify the humour, it is also necessary for the comprehension of most of the participants. Given the dynamism of the pitmatic, its terms continually become outmoded and, ultimately, given the current state of mining, redundant. It is then an antiquated dialect not understood by many, and particularly the younger elderly. In this sense the image of community celebrated is not only one which is idealized, but is, for many of the elderly, in certain respects, part of a past unknown to them, which on entering these contexts they learn about and perpetuate. It is in a sense mythological.

These points, however, only go to serve the main assertion, i.e. that this notion of community is not merely an incidental consequence of the lives of the elderly, but is positively, juxtapositionally constructed. This assumes an intentionality. This intentionality will be evident throughout the book. As I go on to show, the represented and celebrated notion of community is a central feature in the organization of the clubs for the elderly, and it plays a central part in the lives of the elderly, in relation to common transitions and crises implicit in the ageing process.

FOOTNOTES

(1)Themes which arise in this section as central in the characterization of community have been taken up at a theoretical level in what may be termed the 'occupational community debate'. Cole provides a useful guide to the changing nature of this concept of an occupational community (1989:24). The idea of exploitation in explaining solidaristic and co-operative aspects of community life will become evident. The Marxian concepts of exploitation, class conflict, and class based solidarity, are systematically developed by Dennis, Henriques, and Slaughter, as the overriding set of explanatory principles in their classic study of the mining town of Featherstone, which they referred to as Ashton (1956). Perhaps the overriding referent in the characterization of community is mining work itself. This is central to the approach of Henriques, et al, who characterize mining work as the major influence on all life (marriage, family life, political allegiances, religious activity, etc.) within mining communities. Rim-linger (1959:389- 405) has developed this theme in arguing that mining communities are characterized by solidarity and an aggressive separatism and hostility to outsiders who do not face the conditions of mining work. Other approaches include that, for example, of Kerr and Siegel (1954:189-212), who, in their concern to explain the high strike propensity of miners, emphasize the isolation and homogeneity of the condition of mining populations.

Bulmer (1975:61-92) provides a useful set of critiques to a number of these and other such approaches. Having noted this similarity between the themes taken up by the people I worked with, and those developed by a number of writers, it is, however, not my intention to engage in a sociological debate in this context. My concern is merely to outline and discuss the manner in which community is represented in this social context, and discuss its significance in the lives of the people I worked with.

(2)It should be pointed out that this interview took place prior to the Cleveland child abuse case. Nevertheless, on later visits to the field I heard similar comments, as though such negating events could not alter the polarized elements of the characterizations of north and south.

(3)My reference to the symbolic power of coal is entirely restricted to the narrow aims of this section of the book. There are a number of points in this respect which may be developed in a later paper. For example, coal plays a part in rituals symbolizing sexual symmetry. In a ritual which is now outmoded, but which was common in some of the villages, parents delayed the baptism of their child until another child of the opposite sex was born in the village. The parents of this new born child delayed naming it until some member of their family had presented the family of the former child with a piece of coal, and a sweet for that child, at which point the baptism arrangements of this child could then go ahead.

(4)This sub-section has not been developed in the context of the north-south relation due to the sparsity of ethnographic data relating to it. However, the thrust of a number of comments by people I worked with was that perceived southern societal maladies are attributable to the weakness of family structure in that context.

(5)Szurek (1985) has carefully argued that this constant threat, and that women have to cope with an often meagre and, almost always unpredictable income, are fundamental bases for, co-operation and solidarity between women, and the networks of community roles which are a central characteristic of mining communities.

(6)The issue of death will form the basis of future publications.

(7)I intend to dedicate a future paper to an analysis of such taboos, and develop a more comprehensive account of animal classification in this cultural context.

(8)This stereotype is confirmed by Dennis, Henriques, and Slaughter (1956) and criticised later by Frankenberg (1976:25-51).

(9)Themes developed here could be expanded in a later publication. Women's association with death can be developed with reference to a number of aspects of the ethnography. For example, the now outdated extended mourning period for widows, and sexual divisions with respect to contact with the dead. In the system of community roles outlined later women were responsible for dressing the corpse, wailing, and so on. In their book, 'Death and the Regeneration of Life' (1982), Bloch and Parry develop a number of such themes. For example, they discuss such roles and point to women's more benign links with funerary rites.

(10) A detailed analysis of the pitmatic will be covered in a future publication.

(11) See Okely (1983:81) for other commonplace physical items standing as signs of ethnic purity.

(12) I will dedicate a future paper specifically to the question of the hobbies and pastimes that are practiced, and how, in certain respects, they symbolize elements of the social structure and relate to the experience of life in this cultural context.

(13) This practice explains the long standing resistance of miners to accept the N.C.B's insistence on payment by cheque or direct deposit.

(14) For example, one song humorously celebrates the story of Thomas Muckle, who, the song claims, showed the typical quick wit of a mining man by his perfecting a mode of protest (the stopping of moving objects) that was safer than that used by his Morpethian predecessor, Emily Davison. In a protest about women's rights Davison was killed when she threw herself in front of the King's horse. In the 1926 general strike Muckle successfully derailed the Flying Scotsman, which was travelling through the area at full speed, with a train full of passengers.

(15) I am drawing here on Turner's notions of liminality and anti-structure. An early exposition of these notions can be found in his, 'The Ritual Process: Structure and Anti-Structure' (1969), and for developments of these see later publications, such as, 'Dramas, Fields, and Metaphors' (1972:275, 294).

PART III

ISSUES OF THE AGEING PROCESS

This section deals with three interrelated issues of the ageing process. In the first section I discuss a series of culturally constructed notions of the transitions which take place in the ageing process. Secondly, I discuss social differentiation, conflict and association between the elderly. Finally, I consider the perceptions and responses of the elderly to physical and mental decline.

1-TRANSITION AND CONTINUITY IN OLD AGE: CELEBRATION AND RESISTANCE

State defined retirement ages are of little significance in the context of Ashington in terms of their representing a symbolic marker for entry into a new social category, i.e. the aged. Economic exigencies determine the necessity for the outflow from, or influx to, the labour market, which in turn determines the flexibility of retirement policy and, to an extent, notions of when it is socially acceptable for the individual to consider retirement (Phillipson.1982:16-38). However, perhaps more importantly, the decline of the mining industry has led to greater numbers of redundancies and early retirees, and in the case of most women, because of the limited employment opportunities and the fact of the demanding nature of domestic work in the mining family (from which there is often no retirement), lengthy stretches of waged labour are the exception.

Nevertheless, whilst the movement 'from one age to another' by a rite of passage (Van Gennep.1960) may not be clearly marked, specific events, which may or may not be celebrations of retirement, bring into sharp relief the culturally constructed notions of transitions which take place as a part of the ageing process, or the aspects of the person which are seen to persist. In the context of such events these transitions or aspects of the person which are seen to persist may be celebrated, or their resistance may be celebrated. I shall deal with two such events. Interpretation of these will be developed with reference to other general fieldwork data concerning these transitions and the responses of the elderly.

Following the exposition of these events I will deal in turn with three types of transitions and related issues: first, transitions in the sexual identities of the elderly, and their implications for the control of sexuality. Secondly, transitions in the status of the elderly (the term status refers loosely to the distribution of prestige (Lee, et al.1983:179)) and their interdependence and power with respect to younger age groups. Thirdly, I discuss transitions regarding the elderly's contact with previously established social networks, or, the extent and consequences of their marginalization or isolation.

EVENTS

George's retirement party

At the age of 59 George had accepted early retirement when he was offered a good payment by the Coal Board. He had worked in the pit since he was fifteen. Most of those years had been spent as a face worker, but for the last four years he had spent more time on the surface teaching younger miners about safety procedures.

In the afternoon he and two other retirees were called to the manager's office where they were presented with framed long service certificates, and, just before leaving, his immediate boss presented him with a bottle of whisky in front of the staff at the colliery offices. It was a quiet send-off, but more than he had expected. Most men just leave with the certificate and without ceremony. The union's ability to fund and organize retirement celebrations has been seriously affected by the sequestrations which took place during the strike. However, little more could be expected as most of those finishing their service to the industry were leaving with fat redundancy cheques. George was no exception.

Nevertheless, being a drinking man and a regular at the Central Club, his 'marras' had made sure that he would go out in style. His mates from inside and outside the colliery and a lot of the youngsters he had been working with were meeting at the Central straight after they had clocked-off. The plan was to make the celebrations last the weekend; Friday night, Saturday night, and Sunday lunchtime at least. George wasn't to leave until he had been bought a drink by everyone who was to attend. Those clocking-off from different shifts would make sure that if any of the lads peeled-off early there would be a constant supply of replacements to get the beer in. He, however, had other ideas. He had tried not to make a fuss about his retirement and only wanted a small do, but, so as not to be disrespectful, he would at least have one good night. He was aware of the possible consequences of a big do. Jack Turnbull retired on a Friday, drank through to the Sunday, took a heart attack on the Sunday night, and died on the Monday.

On reaching the club, George was greeted with a cheer, and the serious drinking began. His attempts to resist getting drunk failed and when the constant supply of beer began to form into a queue of pint glasses on the table he was goaded to drink up by suggestions that he didn't have the stamina any more to take his beer. The conversation, which was fairly general, but involved some recounting of the yarns about George and his experiences in the pit, dilapidated with the assistance of alcohol. When things became too noisy the management complained and asked the participants to tone things down. This was taken as a cue for antagonizing the management further. Drinks were spilled on the floor and glasses broken, but when this provoked further complaint, participants protested their innocence, tried to move the blame onto George, mockingly castigating him and ordering him to wipe up the mess. At around 10.30 it was announced that there was a surprise in store. However, again mockingly, it was suggested that maybe George had better not stay for it as his wife would be angry about him being late home now that he was an old man, and that she'd be waiting in her sexy nightie to make up for all the lost years he had spent avoiding her at work and down the club. Earlier in the evening a rough cartoon sketch had been passed around the bar. It satirically depicted the amorous advances of George's wife to George in old age.

George's 'new' relationship with his wife was a constant source of fun throughout the evening; she'd stop him going down the club to meet his 'marras', have him going to the Darby and Joan club, and keep him in to do the washing and cleaning. At 11.00 the surprise arrived; a strip-a-gram girl dressed in policewoman's uniform. She asked for George and announced that he was to be arrested for disturbance of the peace and then proceeded to remove her tunic and strip, to the shouts and wolf whistles of the participants, but as George joined in he was removed from his table and taken to the darts room. *"Ee'll hev ney interest in this George....we'll tek you to play a nice quiet game o' darts instead"*, it was jokingly explained. By the time last orders was called

George was covered in beer, dishevelled, virtually unable to walk without assistance, and virtually incomprehensible. He was bundled into a waiting taxi and sent home. The next day people returned, only half expecting to see George. He didn't arrive.

Maggie's birthday party

Maggie worked as a part-time cook at a local school. On the day of her sixty-fifth birthday the other kitchen staff organised a tea party for her. Some of her work mates, knowing what to expect, had declined invitations to the 'real' party which was to be held in the evening.

The 'fancy dress only', 'hen party' in the evening was attended only by women, with the exception of the disc jockey and myself who had been invited along as his assistant and to call the bingo numbers. The women were of all ages; from sixteen to eighty years old, but the greater majority were around Maggie's age. The party was held in the function room of the Excelsior working men's club, upstairs from the bar in which Maggie's husband and some of her friends' husbands were drinking.

The overwhelming characteristic of the celebration was that of the obscene content. The stage for such obscenity was set from the outset. Women came dressed in overtly sexual outfits (for example, French mistresses, bunny girls, etc.). Nevertheless, participation in the obscenity was not general. The very oldest women and the youngest women largely refrained and some of the latter of these expressed some shock. Indeed some of the younger women expressed outrage at seeing their mothers acting in such an undignified manner.

Aided by the alcohol and the goading of the D.J., the obscene content of the women's behaviour became more extreme, from the suggestive lifting of skirts and flashing of underwear, to the photographing of Maggie sucking a cherry tipped banana cocktail, to women utilising French baguettes in highly animated simulation of sexual intercourse. The D.J. and myself increasingly became the foci of comment (for example, invitations to us to become 'toy boys') and gestures (flashing, etc.). We were passive male catalysts of obscenity. The barmaids tried in vain to close the party down when the licence time was exceeded at 11.00, but they were met with a chorus of, *'tek the club, tek the club, tek the club'*. Eventually they called on the club committee to send up some of the husbands from downstairs. When the first of these arrived they were quite literally mobbed and molested, but their mere presence served to bring the party to an abrupt halt and in sharp contrast to the evening's events the women all went home in an orderly and quiet fashion.

SEXUALITY

Transitions in the sexual identities of the elderly

A number of writers have argued that the decline in sexual function of males is more rapid than in that of females (Thienhaus et al.1986:43-44). However, De Beauvoir correctly points to the falsity of the perception of an inextricable link between libido and sexual function (1970:317). Nevertheless, such a link and the former-claim appear to be mirrored in culturally constructed notions and stereotypes of sexual change in old age in this study.

The persistence of the importance of women's sexual identity was explicitly stated on a number of occasions. For example, one woman in her late sixties explained that whilst she had many visitors to her home she felt that the most important of these was the only male friend who visited. She stressed that whilst he was not a boyfriend, "it's nice to knaa that they still think of you, or mebee even think of you that way". The comment stresses the importance of being valued sexually, the possibility that other means by which the woman may he valued may supersede value at this sexual level, but also that the possibility of being valued sexually in old age may persist. At one level the woman's party represented the gathering of women in celebration of their sexual identity.

The events in the men's party went further in

commenting directly on the question of sexual potency. The cartoon (here I fully agree with Hess and Mariner's (1975) assertion that cartoons can be used as an effective means of expressing beliefs and opinions, as they carry familiar symbols of cultural identity) emphasizes the continuity of female sexual potency. On the other hand, both in the cartoon and in the events (George's removal from the room and the erotic pleasures of the strip-a-gram girl to play darts) the elderly man is represented as de-sexualized.

However, this de-sexualization is not represented as a natural consequence of the ageing process in men. The cartoon explains this de-sexualization by utilizing a common stereotype. Harrison (1983) argues that one aspect of the stereotype of elderly women, as constructed by society, defines beauty in relation to the elderly woman. She shows how man's attractiveness is considered to enhance with age, whilst the reverse is considered of women. The cartoon showed George as turned-off and sexually tyrannized by his fat, ugly and wrinkled wife. It conveys the decline of male sexual potency and sexual interest as a response to adverse sexual conditions faced by men in old age, i.e. the declining attractiveness of elderly women.

The contradictory representation of women's sexual identity

The contradiction implicit in the representation of the elderly woman, i.e. continuity of sexual potency alongside declining attractiveness, is reflected in the dominant image of the elderly woman that is celebrated in the clubs for the elderly. In a grotesque juxtaposition between the image of the young sexy woman and the effects of physiological ageing, elderly female strip-tease artists wore oversized bloomers and girdles, and hernia supports, with bunny girl outfits, stilettos, suspender belts and fish net stockings. The sexual identity of men was not a concern and was not celebrated. The same parody of women's sexual identity was the subject of male drag acts. Such acts did not need the accompaniment of words or music. The spectacle of the ugly, yet sexual elderly woman was a sufficient source of hilarity on its own.

Women's sexual humour

The subjects of sex and women's sexual identity are a constant source of conversation between elderly women. However, these concerns are usually conveyed through a humour which appears to encapsulate the ridicule of elderly women implied in the dominant celebrated image of their sexual identity that I go on to explore.

The humour focuses on the body, with salient attention given to breasts and sexual organs, describing them as redundant and dilapidated objects only worthy of derision. For example, one woman commenting on her breasts said, *"Aa wish Aa could hoy them ower me shoulders..... when An walkin' Aa divvent knaa if Aa'm ganna get a black eye or trip ower them"*. On receiving a bottle of sherry in a prize draw a woman commented to her friend, with reference to her vagina, that, *"It'll be just about your size"*. Comments also utilized common stereotypes. For example, one woman commented, on being asked by another to pass a carrier bag to put some raffle tickets, *"I hope you weren't referring to me when you asked for that bag.... will Doris do you?"* The concern with physical decline is implicitly or explicitly linked to the perception of the loss of sexual attractiveness. During a talk given by the police at the Hirst club a woman commented that, *"If any burglar confronts me when Am in bed, Aa'll just say howay on inside son....that'll soon get shot of him"*. Comments which contradict the identification of women as aged and in physical decline, such as women referring to their social group as 'the girls' are also met with hilarity.

This is not simple pleasure giving humour. Its frequency (it is totally pervasive in the conversation of many women) suggests otherwise. Like the strip-tease and drag acts the humour arises from the contradiction in the elderly women's sexual identity. However, unlike the former, women's humour does not display a morbid preoccupation with the ridicule of women, though it is self ridiculing in form. It is a way in which women express the problematic nature of their identity; a covert and repressed expression of its contradictions.

Sexual relations of the elderly

Generally speaking most people I spoke to suggested that the cessation of sexual activity in old age was normal. The possibility of the continuity of sexual relations inside marital relationships was never spoken of, but it was widely accepted that there was a very limited degree of non-marital sexual liaison between elderly people. Such behaviour was clearly viewed as deviant.

The elderly are reminded in this respect by the descriptions of such liaison. People were not concerned with pointing to where such contact might actually take place, but, rather, presented exaggerated descriptions of a series of arenas which served to heighten the deviant label. Prominent amongst these are the allotments (a dirty and smelly place only fit for the mating pigs who live there) and the 'grab a Grannie' night at the Universal club. My experience of the latter somewhat undermines its description as a seedy pick-up joint. Elderly men and women, including both single people and couples, meet once a week in the club to engage in some old-time dancing. Interaction at the event appeared to contain no more, and perhaps less, of a sexual content than in the clubs for the elderly.

Gender differences in the deviant labels

Whilst sexuality in old age generally is considered deviant, the labels attached to, and derogatory remarks directed at, women suspected of showing an interest in, or actually engaging in, sexual activity are unquestionably negative, whereas the converse is the case with men. Such women were openly referred to as, for example, 'W.H.O.R.E.S.' and 'slags' (a term with added poignancy in this particular cultural context where the waste by-products of mining are symbolically represented as particularly polluting). Women run the risk of attracting such labels and remarks in all female, as well as mixed gender, contexts. Even in the women's retirement party other women were scathingly critical of the sexual content of the behaviour of Maggie and her peers.

In all male contexts sex is accepted as an unproblematic subject for conversation. Even in contexts where different age groups participate, it is a common topic of conversation which crosses the generational divide. Moreover, in the Buffs and in the working men's clubs some older men talked about, and in some cases boasted of their virility or their voyeuristic exploits quite openly, and the various descriptions of, and deviant labels attached to such men, ('dorty owld buggers', or 'mac flashers', etc.) possessed not a hint of negative connotation. On the contrary, the perceived sexual content of their behaviour was jovially referred to as indicative of their qualities of endurance (1).

It is insufficient to explain this dichotomy in terms of connotations attached to women's sexuality generally. Any explanation must take into account the culturally constructed ageing process in this social context. A number of comments by the people encountered suggested that the sexuality of elderly women is problematic in a number of respects. These can be summarized as follows. There is a sense in which female sexuality in old age is considered deviant because of an underlying moral precept associating sex and procreative potential. Secondly, the perceived disparity between men and women in terms of sexual potency is seen to enhance the potential sexual availability of elderly women. It could be argued that this represents a threat to a morally desirous world of sexual monogamy. Finally, Harrison (1983) points out that the result of the perception of women's decreasing attractiveness with age is that women are considered sexually ineligible. This idea, above all, was repeated by the people I worked with.

The precarious identity of the elderly woman

The continuing importance of women's sexual identity and the perception of women's continued sexual potency, alongside the identification of sexuality in old age as deviant and, more particularly, the perception of elderly women as sexually ineligible, because of their declining attractiveness, attributes elderly women with, not only a contradictory identity, but one that is also, in a sense, precarious. This point is exemplified by an incident which took place on the return leg of a bus trip to Seahouses (after some of the participants had stopped off for a few drinks) which was organized by and for the members of the North Seaton club.

Two of the participants, Hilda (who was fondly regarded as the comedienne of the club) and another Hilda (who was seen as an intruder and was widely disliked), who were both in semi-drunken states, attempted to amuse the others on the coach. Their entertainment was of a largely sexual nature; mock fondling of other women, stroking the driver's head, and Hilda the comedienne singing a song entitled, 'Come home with me darling or me poor little pussy will be alone once more'. The sexual content in the actions of each woman appeared to be no more severe than in those of the other. Nevertheless, whilst Hilda the comedienne was laughed at and appreciated, the other woman's actions merely served to provoke whispered critical comments; one woman called her a whore and another woman suggested that it wasn't surprising that her husband had died as she'd probably worn him out with her insatiable sexual appetite. The criticism was not provoked by any background information or suspicion about the woman's sex life.

The incident shows that even where the dominant image of the sexual identity of women in old age is conformed to, the criticism and invocation of labels of deviant sexuality may be no less vehement. These labels are arbitrarily used in the denigration of women who are disliked. It is in this sense that the elderly woman can be characterized as possessing a precarious identity. The elderly woman is represented as constantly bordering on the edge of a deviant identity.

Control of sexuality in the social arenas of the elderly

The clubs for the elderly are characterized by a sexually charged ambience. Much mixed gender socializing has a sexual content. Indeed, for example, people reminisced of the Saturday night dances where men sat with men and women sat with women, discussing the 'talent' and the risks involved in making the first, highly ritualized, mechanical and courteous moves. There is an extent to which such conventions are carried into the contexts of the clubs for the elderly where, after all, because of the large number of single people there is a high degree of 'potential' sexual availability. Moreover, for some of the participants the clubs represent a break from their pasts where socializing in the community beyond the family was largely done in exclusively male or female contexts. The sexual content developed in interactions in these previous contexts is often carried into the new mixed gender context.

The sexual content can usually be described as humorously suggestive. Absent members were accused of eloping, people were teased about showing interest in members of the opposite sex, mock plans were laid for couples to date or elope, conversations were interrupted by others who interpreted conversational elements as being sexually suggestive, groups of women were referred to by others as man-killers, and so on. On some, usually celebratory, occasions where alcohol was available, the play did go somewhat further. For example, women sat on men's knees, pampered them, kissed them, and stroked their heads. Such extension of the sexual content was usually instigated by women but some men were compliant.

Up to such a point the behaviour was generally accepted, but anything exceeding this was scorned and controlled. It is difficult to define the boundaries of acceptable sexual behaviour, but, generally speaking, actions or comments which could be interpreted as amounting to a real expression of sexual desire or intent are taboo.

Women are keenly aware of the high risk of being labelled, particularly by adversaries, with the derogatory identifications of sexual deviance. Consequently they took care to whisper, either to me, or to close friends, any comments which could be interpreted as amounting to a real expression of sexual desire, and moderate actions which might have a similar effect. The power of gossip as a form of sexual sanction was all too evident.

Control at other levels was dramatically exemplified by the reception given to a concert party act at the Ellington club. Two women wearing grass skirts danced to the Hawaiian music performed by the concert party band. One of the women was large and used her size as the prime focus of her act; shaking and rolling her body and protruding her stomach, backside and breasts. Her exaggerated movements were intended to provoke laughter. The other woman, however, did not deem it inappropriate to display an air of desirability. She danced seriously and seductively.

The reactions of the audience were dramatically split in relation to the two. They laughed heartily at the first woman's antics and joined in the fun; women stood up to dance with her and men blew her kisses and invited her to sit on their knees. Some people laughed at the other woman, some were scathingly critical, and men nervously moved away from her and often violently refused her attempts to give them a rose or kiss them.

The event and audience reaction served to lay bare the extent to which control is generated in these contexts and showed how the celebration of the dominant image of the elderly woman serves in this control. As stated before, this image (conformed to and exaggerated by the first woman) emphasizes the continuity of the elderly woman's sexual potency and her declining attractiveness, i.e. it is a contradictory image involving grotesque juxtaposition. In emphasizing the elderly woman's declining attractiveness, it reasserts her sexual ineligibility. The humorous exaggeration of the contradictory elements (implicit in the display of the first woman) merely adds to the rendering of the idea of the elderly woman's participation in sexual relations as a grotesque absurdity.

In this sense the event served to exemplify the boundaries and definition of acceptable sexual behaviour for elderly women, i.e. behaviour stripped of any seriousness. By displaying a degree of eroticism and desirability, the second woman not only subverted this dominant image, but, in doing so, overstepped these boundaries herself, portraying a serious and unridiculed image of her sexual identity. This explains the castigating element in the audience reaction.

A corollary of this image of the elderly woman's sexual identity is that sexual relations between the elderly generally are rendered as an absurdity. Indeed, this is also implied by the cartoon. The audience reaction can also be understood in relation to this. By the serious appearance of her display, the second woman presented the possibility for people to show that they may harbour sexual feelings towards such elderly women. In this sense the audience reaction was, in part, engendered by a fear of being seen to harbour such feelings. Thus, events in the clubs serve to engender, not only control of women's sexuality, but control of the sexuality of the elderly generally.

Acquiescence and resistance to the dominant image of the elder women

In many cases the women who participated in such acts were not random. It was often those who, above all others, were perceived to harbour sexual desires and who displayed a degree of sexual content in their behaviour who were encouraged to participate in these acts. One of the club leaders told me straightforwardly that the acts gave the women a chance to channel their pent-up desires; "*t' get it oot've them*". This suggests, it can be argued, that, firstly, such women were, ultimately, unwitting agents in their own control, and, secondly, their encouragement represented a form of punishment (i.e. in relation to their former transgressions of these boundaries). The very least that can be said is that they were encouraged to indulge in what was, and effectively recognized as such by many of the club participants, an act of degrading self ridicule.

Nonetheless, specific acts can be interpreted as acts of resistance to the dominant image of the elderly woman. The dancing of the second woman can be characterized as such. I have said that she effectively subverted the dominant image of the elderly woman and portrayed a serious and un-ridiculed image of her own sexual identity. In certain respects the events in the woman's party can be similarly interpreted. However, that the events quickly terminated when men entered is indicative of the fact that such an open and, to an extent, aggressive celebration of an un-ridiculed sexual identity could only take place under specific conditions. The stage was set from the outset in a number of ways. It was stimulated by the choice of costumes. In the near absence of men and the total absence of men of a similar age, the risk of being seen to harbour sexual intentions towards a participant was reduced. In the presence of close friends the risk of invocation of derogatory sexual slander was minimal (though not absent). The presence of close friends and the fact that it was a party gave licence to a sexual content in the celebrations. The ribaldry was aided generally by alcohol, etc.

Conclusions

Representations of the sexual elements of the transition into the category of the aged involve the perceptions of declining male sexual potency and the continuity of female sexual potency, alongside a perception of the fading attractiveness of the elderly woman. Secondly, sexual relations of the elderly are considered deviant, but whilst the sexuality of the elderly woman is attributed with negative connotations, the converse is the case for the elderly man. The primary reason for this dichotomy is this perception of women's declining attractiveness, which renders her as sexually ineligible.

The contradiction implicit in the elderly woman's identity (i.e. continued sexual potency - declining attractiveness) is of primary significance in a number of respects. Women's humour, which is imbued with a sexual content, represents a repressed expression of this contradiction. One consequence of this contradiction (alongside the facts that women's sexual identity remains important within their lives, and they are considered sexually ineligible) is that the elderly woman is constantly bordering on the edge of a deviant sexual identity. Most importantly, the main contradiction informs the dominant image of the elderly woman that is celebrated in the clubs for the elderly. This image is not merely a source of humour (humour which flows from the exaggeration of this contradiction); it is a key element in the control of the elderly with respect to sexuality. It reasserts the ineligibility of the elderly woman. Moreover, its exaggeration in the club contexts renders, not only the idea of the elderly woman's participation in sexual relations as an absurdity, but, by implication, sexual relations between the elderly generally. I have also emphasized that the sexual identity of elderly women remains important in their lives, and that specific acts can be interpreted as resistance to, and subversion of this dominant ridiculing image, and a reassertion and celebration of an un-ridiculed sexual identity.

Finally, I have implied that there was an aggressive element in the sexual content of the women's behaviour in the birthday party (the advances to myself and the D.J. and the '*tekkin*' of the club). Such actions drew on imagery of elderly women's sexual potency and a power disparity between men and women which stems from the perception of a disparity between elderly men and women in terms of sexual potency. This disparity was explicit in the portrayal of the domineering wife in the cartoon and in comments made at the man's retirement party. With respect to the women's party it should be pointed out that the word to 'tek' has numerous meanings; to occupy, to take possession of, and, most importantly in this context, to take sexual control over someone. However, this 'tekkin' of the club and representation of such a power disparity in the men's event are more significant in another context. I argue below how such imagery relating to sexual transitions comments on other representations of the transitions of the ageing process, and questions of gender rather than sexuality.

ROLES AND STATUS

MEN

People frequently spoke of the loss of the, *'owld style Grandad'*, and complained that respect for the elderly had diminished. This is one element of the general perception of moral and social decline. First, the diminution of respect may be explained by the recent massive growth of the number of retirees. Whereas elderly retired men were once the exception, and attained prestige because of this rarity and the perception that they possessed powers of endurance necessary to survive a full productive life in the pit, they now constitute one of the larger parts of Ashington's population. Secondly, within the area the relations between old and young upon which such respect may have been based have been undermined as a consequence of the run-down of the mining industry and changes in the organisation of mining production.

It was explained to me that the cavel system engendered the partial dependence of young upon old, based upon the power and knowledge of elders in the mining context. The skills and knowledge of mining were learnt within the teams from the elder members, or, where young men worked as individual hewers or datal workers anticipating promotion to the cavel, passed from elders in conversation generally or in advice given at the pit face. Secondly, elders were always responsible for choosing new members for their teams, and were also largely responsible for the recruitment of new workers by the company. To an extent, through the deputies and oversmen, the mining companies usually sought the advice and accepted the recommendations of long-term employees with respect to the recruitment of new workers. Even after retirement, elderly men often maintained a link with the industry, passing on some of the knowledge required to younger members of their family, and more importantly, through their acquaintance with people at the colliery, they were able to continue to act as kingmakers in the employment of younger members to the teams.

The favour of employment was, it was explained to

me, often reciprocated, such that elderly members were allowed by the others to remain in the teams, retaining employment well beyond a respectable level of efficient productive capacity. As it was explained to me, younger miners often used to, *'carry the aad uns'*. However this was so not just because of reciprocity. Older members maintained decision making power in the team because of their experience, and, more interestingly, pressure for their continued employment often came from within the community or the family. The latter was possible because much recruitment was done within families, such that in some cases the representatives of up to three generations of a family could be employed in one team.

Changes in the industry have involved deskilling, the centralization of training, the diminishment of teamwork extraction, and the introduction of a system of direct company recruitment which is largely free of nepotism. These have served, effectively, to eradicate these sources of dependency and the bases of what can be described as patriarchal knowledge and power. Moreover, the declining numbers of younger people going into the industry and the increasing level of out-migration make such power and knowledge impotent and irrelevant from the outset. The deprivation, through the decreasing significance of their knowledge and the eradication of their kingmakers employment role, of the possibility of the elderly men maintaining power is mirrored in a diminution of their status.

Elements of the retirement celebration reflected this

diminution of status. Whilst in the hierarchical employment structure of the pit, George (the retiree) had been senior to many of the participants, in the context of the retirement party this was, at least symbolically, overturned. His strength was put to the test in competition with younger men (i.e. through the heavy drinking which was set to last the whole weekend), positions of authority were reversed (i.e. he was made accountable for the mess the other men created, and was ordered to clear it up), and throughout, he was systematically humiliated (embodied in the end by his being rendered drunken, incapable, unintelligible, and dishevelled). At one level the events can be read as a ritual of reversal where the status and power order of working hierarchies are temporarily inverted. Even in relation to a retirement celebration this interpretation may have been valid in the pre-cavel era, but, given changes in the mining industry that I have outlined, the events represent the transition into retirement where the elderly initiate is seen to be permanently stripped of power, and, consequentially, partially because of his loss of a productive role, represented as socially inferior. The event was, in effect, an inversion of initiation.

Hockey and James have argued that the elderly are often made, metaphorically, to assume a child-like status (1988). Such infantalization typifies the manner in which the elderly men in this context are stripped of status. The manner in which people spoke of the allotment users utilized vocabulary which would normally be descriptive of childhood ("*that's where the owld uns get up to their tricks*", "*ee spends ees time pottering aboot doon at the allotment*", etc.), as though they were an oversized playpen.

Elsewhere I have noted that the allotments have attained a deviant status (i.e. the arena of illicit sexual relations). This is evoked again, but this time in a manner which crystallizes this cultural infantalization of elderly men. The elderly users of the allotments often grow more than they can eat. Parents send their children to the allotments with a few coppers to buy some of this excess. The old men give the vegetables to the children for free and tell them to take the money, which their parents wouldn't directly allow them to have, to spend on 'bullets' (sweets) at the corner shop. Everyone, including the parents are aware of what happens to the money, but with the children maintain the facade of ignorance. The act is one of recognised and, indeed, encouraged mutual complicity between old and young. The two age groups are represented as symbolic peers. As a corollary of this, what is inappropriate for children is also inappropriate for the elderly. I noted earlier that the events in the retirement party served to emphasize the inappropriateness of sexual enjoyment for the elderly. This perception of inappropriateness must also be understood in terms of the infantalization of the elderly as well as in terms of the representations of the sexual transitions involved in the ageing process. The de-sexualized old man is akin to the pre-sexualized child. It is by no means coincidental that the participants emphasized that the playing of a game was a more suitable form of enjoyment for the elderly man than the erotic pleasures of the strip-a-gram girl.

Aspects of the culturally constructed identity of the elderly man thus stress declining status and power as a result of worthlessness in the context of industrial changes. However, the men I worked with cannot be regarded as passive recipients of such identification. Specific acts can be interpreted as resistance.

Firstly, many of the men maintain an intimate attachment to the culture of work. The clubs are particularly important in facilitating this. Much of the interaction in the clubs is about the pit. As meeting places for working and retired miners (though this aspect of club life is diminishing), the latter are able (if they have access to such a club) to keep in touch with developments at the pit. The contrast between pit work in the present and in 'their day' is a constant source of conversation and argument. Even club events refer to pit work. For example, I witnessed quiz games in which the questions concerned issues such as the rules and procedures of pit safety and coal extraction techniques. At one level the continued attachment to the culture of work seems to be no more than an inevitable maintenance of an interest in a subject that has been a central concern throughout their lives. However, a previous use of the clubs was as centres of employment broking. In this sense the practices outlined above can perhaps be seen as an impotent reflection of the playing out of the king-maker role of the elderly men which has been denied them because of changes.

Finally, of course, an important consequence of the increasing levels of redundancy and early retirement, and the reduction of statutory age limits on employment has been the diminution of potential continuation of employment for the growing elderly sector of the population. As if in denial of any assumption that retirement from waged labour may imply redundancy, some of the men I spoke to characterized retirement as another phase in their working lives. Activities such as increased participation in family life and, indeed, gardening were described as work. In the case of the latter, the extent to which perceived status may have been undermined by the loss of a 'productive' role provided by work is resisted in the sense that gardening is in itself productive, and, moreover, it is often explicitly recognized as a means of achieving prestige. The institutionalized expression of this is the organized 'growing for showing' associations and competitions(2).

WOMEN

Few of the women I worked with had been employed in long term waged labour and almost none had considered themselves to have been the main breadwinner within their family. In contradistinction to men, productivity and financial provision played a minor part in women's self evaluation. As noted earlier in the book the central bases for the evaluation of women relate to supportive domestic roles within the family and, to a lesser degree, caring and organizational roles within the wider community structure.

As in the case of men, women complained of the diminution of respect for the elderly generally and the disappearance of an archetypal matriarchal grandmother figure. In addition to the point about the growth of the elderly population, one reason for this diminution must be the fact that elderly women have been largely deprived of these active roles in the community, displaced by the growth of the welfare state and undermined by the breakdown of the community as they see it. However, with respect to their position within the family, except in the sense that immediate influential contact with relatives has in many cases been denied by the level of outmigration, there seem to be few tangible bases upon which industrial change might have brought about this diminution. Secondly, one can only speculate about how ideological changes may have undermined respect and matriarchal roles. Ideological changes have obviously had their effect. They may at least partially account for the disagreements elderly women I worked with had with their younger families, as aspects of matriarchal knowledge were brought into question. Nevertheless, most of the women I worked with claimed that they maintained good relations with their families and performed active caring and advisory roles in this context. Indeed, to an extent, such disagreements are in themselves indicative of this.

However, this is not to suggest that the elderly women are not in any way negatively represented and seen as diminished in actual importance. Note the rendering of women's sexuality as a joke. Furthermore, a series of negative stereotypes about women will become evident throughout the book.

Nevertheless, it is this supportive domestic role which women refer to in resistance to such denigrating stereotypes. This was most dramatically exemplified in a struggle between the organizers of the Ellington day centre and two representatives from its umbrella organization. Age Concern sent down two new voluntary helpers to gain some experience and help out in the centre. They were alarmed at the level of inactivity.

The old women just sat around drinking tea, playing cards, dominoes, or bingo, and chatting. They confided in me that this was perhaps not surprising. The club leader and her friends had run the club for fifteen years. They were older than most of the members. They planned to 'ease a bit of the strain' on her, and 'inject a bit of life into the place'. They also explained, quoting from an Age Concern leaflet, that they hoped to make the participants aware of their potential value to the community. They could show them that their knowledge of dying handicraft skills could be passed on to the younger members of the community, and thus used as an educational asset. They intended to make a start on this at the next day centre meeting.

The following week they returned armed with scissors, glue, old greeting cards, cotton wool, and a bag of old toilet rolls (the ultimate insult and metaphor for uselessness; something to be disregarded and recycled). The elderly women were going to make some pretty collages to decorate the hall in time for the visit of the local school children who were putting on a show for them. The members grudgingly complied and the club leader with some of her team agreed to take a break from the general organizational and kitchen work to help out the others in the collage making.

As the weeks went by, the members became progressively discontented. The voluntary workers had offended at two levels. Though many of the members were bored by the constant games of bingo and so on, the new pursuits were seen as particularly infantile. Secondly, members were unhappy about the helpers subversion of the organization of the centre. The centre was partially dependent on the help of young volunteers, both directly, for example, they used the services of a young driver, and indirectly, for example, the centre was dependent on the financial assistance of Age Concern whose existence is largely dependent on the work of young volunteers. However, in the domestic aspect of the centre's organization, the relationship between old and young was seen and presented as equal. This was further reinforced by the lack of boundaries between organizers and members. Organizers (both old and young) joined in the leisure pursuits, and members were allowed to help out with the cooking, serving of meals, washing up and so on. Not only had the volunteers erected boundaries which dissuaded members' participation in the cooking of meals and the general running of the club, but they had also served to divide the younger and older organizers. The leader was effectively displaced.

This situation went on for three weeks until the week after the children's show. When the voluntary workers arrived they went to the kitchen to prepare lunch for the day. However, a special Christmas feast had already been prepared. Each tray contained a turkey salad, trifle for afters, a glass of sherry, a Christmas cracker, and a small gift. The leader insisted that the volunteers should be given V.I.P treatment. They were sat at the head table and served by the other helpers and participants who went to great lengths to make sure they did not have to do anything for themselves. Afterwards a grand bingo session was held where the ticket prices were raised from ten to fifty pence a book. One of the elderly helpers was sent off to the shop with the proceeds from the bingo, and returned later with three large gift-wrapped boxes of chocolates. One of the boxes was given to the first woman to win two of the bingo games and the other two were presented to the two voluntary workers. The leader publicly thanked them for the big improvements they had brought to the club and, to the surprise of both the members and the volunteers, who had expected the volunteers to stay on, she gave them her best wishes for their future with Age Concern and said that if they wished to drop in from time to time they would be made most welcome. They were warmly applauded. After the members had washed the dishes and cleared up the hall in a collective effort, and had left, the volunteers told the leader that there had been a misunderstanding. They intended to return after the Christmas recess. The leader said that this fact had completely slipped her mind. She was becoming a bit forgetful in her old age.

The members celebrated their abilities as cooks, caterers and hosts, and the events served to restate the nature of the relationship between old and young and the boundaries of dependence and independence of the elderly in this context. The making and serving of the meal and the clearing up afterwards restated the independence of the members in the sphere of domestic organization. The participation of both members generally and younger volunteers, to the exclusion of the new volunteers, emphasized the equality of the relationship between old and young in this context. The extravagance of the meal served to illustrate the efficacy of this form of organization and the capabilities of the elderly participants in looking after this side of the centre's events. The praise which was heaped upon the two women, partially reflecting this dependence on young volunteers, was an expression of genuine gratitude for their charity. Nevertheless, the V.I.P. treatment was a kind of 'potlach' or imbalanced reciprocity/hostility (Mauss, 1954). The treatment could not be returned and the volunteers were effectively humiliated, defined as mere 'guests', and, essentially, intruders. This, and the leader's 'error' served to lay the way for their departure.

After the Christmas recess, the voluntary workers did not return, the craft equipment was put away in the cupboard and the normal day centre activities resumed. I was not able to become aware of what happened behind the scenes between the leader, the voluntary workers, and Age Concern, and discover the reasons for the women's departure. However, the leader's retrospective comments left me in no doubt she had responded to the feelings of disgruntled members and had been instrumental in ensuring the helper's departure. She stated, in a righteous tone as if she had acted for the best, "*they were lovely, well meaning girls, but the ladies like their cards and bingo*". If this is the case then it is clear that she used and overplayed the perceived weaknesses of her age (i.e. her claim to have forgotten that the women were to stay on after Christmas) as an asset/weapon in securing the ends she desired. However, the leader's failure to divulge information about the nature of the departure of the two women left a feeling among the members that the dinner had been an effective act of resistance on the part of the members generally.

The denigration of the elderly members and its resistance was implicit in the concrete actions of old and young, where access to specific roles upon which personal value is largely based were at stake. Moreover, denigration was also implicit in the helpers' invocation of a series of negatively stereotypical images of the elderly; for example, passivity and declining intellectual ability (their critique of bingo was based on the assumption that the members should be mentally stimulated in more active and taxing ways), and infantalization (the making of decorations for visiting children). In themselves these also provoked the antagonism of the elderly participants.

In most cases awareness of potential denigration relates to such images. People frequently spoke of a fear of being negatively perceived by others. The comments of one elderly woman I worked with expressed this awareness.

"Am always frightened people's watchin' us. They'll think there's something on. They'll mebee think Aa've got a disease with me shufflin' aboot an that. Aa always think folks is lookin', so Aa divvent gan oot that much. That's what stops us."

This awareness is not, of course an exclusively female phenomenon. However, the comments and actions of women are particularly interesting in that they bring into relief the central role of the family in women's resistance of such images.

In restatement of personal value in defensive contradistinction to the threat of being seen by others, or even by themselves, as conforming to these images, the women frequently take the opportunity to introduce and proudly display members of their family in the club contexts. Family monologues serve a similar function. These are frequently introduced into conversations at often completely incongruous ways to the general nature and subject. The significance of the family is that it is, for most of the women, the symbol of the successful execution of their supportive domestic role.

The family is also used and referred to in a much more abstract sense, more in order to deflect the potential perception of being seen to conform to these images rather than, as is the case above, to defensively contradict these images. This was clearly evident in the nature of interactions which took place both during and after a shopping trip which was arranged for the members of the Ellington day centre.

I spent most of the day with a group of three of the women from the centre and a young female helper from a local hospital. The three elderly women wanted to split away from the main group and spend the day with me and the helper. They expressed distaste at the idea of staying with the others, not so much because of any conflicts or dislikes, but because they just didn't want to be seen with them. For example, Doris said she didn't want people looking at her thinking that she had just been, "*carted oot of the hospital with aall the other patients.*" We started off the visit by calling in at a cafe where it was agreed that the helper and I looked sufficiently similar to be regarded by others as brother and sister. They argued about who could look most like our mother, and after some time it was agreed that people in the shopping centre would think we were a family.

The events which had started in the shopping centre were continued in a new form for a number of weeks after in the context of the centre. Throughout the day at the shopping centre the women had offered to buy the helper and myself a variety of items (tea, sweets, etc.). This heralded the beginning of a period of competitive gift buying until the end of the day centre term. Moreover, I became a kind of make believe surrogate son. Doris told me that she would be happy if I was her son, and Hilda said that she tells her flatmate that she comes to the centre to see her other boy.

In the first context the imaginative construction of the family group was explicitly designed to deflect the potentially negative gaze of the other. It was used to distance themselves from the other elderly and deflect the label of institutionalized, the negative connotations of which were seen as self evident. In the second case the constructed situation was moved to an arena where others were of lesser significance. In this case the concern was to deflect potential self awareness of conformity to these negative images. The actions represented a symbolic reordering of the environment; an environment perceived as negatively abnormal, i.e. their placement in the old people's centre as one of its 'patients' was rectified into an idealized normality, i.e. their situation within a family scene.

CONCLUSIONS

First, the identities of men and women and the means by which they are valued are inseparably linked to their respective career roles, which in this area have been clearly historically marked by a rigid division of labour.

Secondly, in contradistinction to men who are, and are seen to be, stripped of their major (productive/economic) role, women's passage into the social category of aged is, by and large, characterized by a perceived and/or actual continuity of role. Also, of course, in a sense, many women do retire from such roles, i.e. withdrawal from active participation in family life through choice, illness, or other such reasons, but in contradistinction to the suddenness of men's withdrawal from waged mining work, within a relatively narrow age range, in the case of women, such withdrawal cannot usually be characterized as a sudden rupture at a legally or other specified moment in the life span.

Despite the difference between men and women outlined above, resistance by elderly men and women alike to their negative representation and treatment usually draws upon their respective working roles (men's maintained attachment to a culture of work, the women's resistance to their marginalization and denigration to the status of cared-for and controlled 'patients' within the club by their establishing the right to perform domestic tasks, etc.) I do not, however, include in this their responses to the representation of their sexual identity, which I have dealt with separately.

One final point concerns the attribution of negative and demeaning connotations to the leisure arenas used by the elderly (for example, the allotments as places for the old men to 'potter about' and the day centre as a place filled with 'patients'). The elderly participants regard for such contexts is often, not surprisingly, characterized by ambivalence. Recognition of them as providing essential social contact is held alongside awareness that participation presents the danger of the person having the labels applied to the context thrust upon him/herself by others. For example, Doris was aware of being seen as a patient and reacted by distancing herself from the group within which she was a participant. In another sense the participants are aware of self conformity to their own negatively stereotypical conceptions about the life of the elderly. Similarly, distancing is often the reaction, but within the context and amongst peers, where outsiders are of no significance. For example, participants operate such categories as the old/old and young/old. Such categories often relate to actual age differences, but may also be based upon arbitrary criteria such as appearance, lifestyle, taste, and so on. For example one woman at the Northumberland Close club told me that the problem with the club was that the old ones liked the bingo too much, when in fact there was no generational divide in relation to preferred leisure activities. If there was a divide at this level it was, rather, one of class. The main point is that participants positively define themselves in contradistinction to other elderly. A consequence is that the type of negative perceptions of the elderly outlined above operates amongst the elderly themselves and is to an extent exacerbated. This in itself is a source of tension in such contexts, and when such categories are articulated at a practical level, where, for example, participants attempt to establish cared and cared-for relationships, which contravene principles of self help, as I discuss later. The result is often open conflict.

ISOLATION AND MARGINALITY

MEN

The men I spoke to differentially described how retirement and ageing had affected their ability (where it was desired) to maintain the gender differentiated nature of their leisure pursuits. Some men described their activities as acts of avoidance of the home necessitated because their wives regarded their presence as cumbersome and interfering, not just in relation to the execution of domestic tasks, but also in relation to the women's social networks, which had been built up around the home. The common site of old men standing in groups together on street corners is comically, though perhaps accurately, described and depicted as a reflection of their banishment from the home. Conversely, others suggested that retirement had led to unwanted pressure from their wives to participate more in home life or socialize more as couples, and claimed that they took refuge from this in the allotments or the clubs.

Perception of the allotments and clubs as arenas which are out of bounds for women allow this possibility. In the case of the allotments none of the patches are let out to women. This is not so because legislation prevents it or because gardening is unpopular amongst women. The allotments are widely perceived as a male domain, inappropriate for women to use or even fleetingly visit. In their otherwise useful work on allotments, Ward and Crouch (1988) failed to find this gender dimension. This is buttressed by common rumours and ideas whose consequence is that women visitors to the allotments risk the potential stigma of sexual promiscuity. As I have noted, the allotments are cited as an arena for illicit sexual liaison. Moreover, it was explained to me that women who 'want a bit of adventure' approach men with the request for some form of produce from the allotments. On delivery or collection of the produce the women have sex with the giver as a form of payment, either in the allotment shed or in the woman's home if her husband is away. Others doubted the validity of the tale (especially the barter element) or the fact that the allotments were used in this way at all. Nevertheless, the commonly cited term, 'the dozen eggs women', used to describe promiscuous women, whose origin lies in this type of account of sexual contact and use of the allotments, serves to reinforce the perception of the allotments as out of bounds for women.

This perception is also perhaps reinforced by the appearance of the allotments. In many respects they resemble a shanty town. Fences, sheds, and greenhouses are improvised structures made from materials obtained by every means other than purchase to specification. The anarchic effect is heightened by the level of bad craftsmanship (the reasons for bad craftsmanship stem, it was suggested to me, from the rigid sexual division of labour, which involved women being responsible for all tasks in the home, including the home maintenance work which is now widely regarded as a task for men). In this respect they stand in sharp contrast to the ordered image of the home and domestic environment, which, as I have argued, is represented in symbolized notions of space as the domain of women.

The suggestion that the allotments are used as a refuge in the manner outlined is perhaps exemplified by the fact that many men leave their plots uncultivated, but come in all weather with sandwiches, transistor radios and newspapers, to spend the whole day in the peace of their shed. Indeed some of the women I spoke to talked of their husbands as almost living in the allotments.

In the case of the clubs, though there is no official ban on women, many of the clubs are, like the allotments, essentially the domain of men. Women often visit, but sit in the lounge. They neither enter nor are accepted in the bar. The inaccessibility of these to women is further reinforced by the nature of interaction in the bar area, which is only fully intelligible to men of the area. Much of the subject matter (for example, mining), and form (for example, a conflictual form that I explore later) of conversation between men, and the language (i.e. as noted earlier, much of the pitmatic is alien to women) in which it is expressed, is alien to women.

However, reflecting the gender differentiated social spheres outlined at the outset, many men and women I worked with also explained that they had developed little in common concerning their ideas of leisure, and by mutual consent maintained the divided social lives that had existed in the pre-retirement years. However, for such men the clubs remain important. They represent much more than impenetrable strongholds of male working culture. Most importantly, the clubs are alternative centres for advice on a whole range of issues, from gardening, to health problems, and financial matters. People come to the clubs with the intention of finding out information which in some cases could more directly and accurately have been gathered from conventional and official sources.

Thus withdrawal from the clubs represents more than a curtailment of leisure activity. It is to an extent tantamount to social isolation, or, in other words, social death. Given both the location of male and female social networks and the fact of the industrial changes outlined in the previous section, this threat is greater in the case of elderly men than it is for women. Since many elderly people are affected by the problem of reduced mobility, the threat of isolation appears greater in the case of men because of their usual need to travel in order to maintain their social links (i.e. explained by the fact that male social networks have tended to develop around the pit where the majority of the working men's clubs also tend to be concentrated, whereas women's social networks tend to be situated around the home). It should be noted that whilst the roles that elderly men once had guaranteed their integration in cross-generational contexts of socializing, the stripping of these roles, in combination with a series of other ideological and structural changes, has led to their marginality in this sense. The elderly users of the working men's clubs have been forced into using an ever decreasing rump of 'male only' working men's clubs where the membership is decreasingly cross-generational and increasingly aged. In response to the changing tastes of younger and wealthier clients, the clubs are, increasingly, welcoming both men and women and introducing other changes which do not suit older male clients (video machines, loud music, etc.).

The allotments stand as a potent symbol of such marginality. For a number of reasons (for example, newer accommodation tends to have garden space, the movement towards privatism, and the fact that the elderly have more leisure time) the allotments tend to be used more by the elderly. On one side they border the field where the other retirees from the pit, the pit ponies, have been put out to grass, and at the front they are

enclosed by a high wooden fence, to protect the residents from the eye-sore
(i.e. the allotments' shanty town appearance) which is felt may affect their property prices.

The significance of the events in the retirement party directly relate to this question of isolation. At one level the events can be read as representing a change in the power relationship between man and wife involved in the act of the man's retirement. For example, retirement entails the man's loss of economic and political power through the loss of the wage packet. The sexual imagery has another significance in this sense. The loss of male sexual potency can be seen as representing his loss of power generally, and the representation of the sexual tyranny of the elderly man by his wife can be seen as representing the new power disparity between them that results from the transition to retirement.

Results of this new power relationship were explicitly referred to. His wife would force him to make up for lost years in all senses; sexual, social, and in a new division of domestic work. Moreover, these were explicitly represented as entailing the man's withdrawal from his previously established, predominantly male social spheres. Thus, the image of the pressurizing and sexually dominant women in the retirement celebration stands as a cultural representation of man's potential isolation.

Two important points should be made about this explanation of the events. First, the events contained the element of humiliation associated with rites of passage. Usually this has been pointed to in studies concerned with re-joining and initiation into social groups (see, for example, Van Gennep (1960) and Goffman's (1961) remarks on the stripping of identity which I will comment upon later). In this case they are associated with the symbolic dispatch from the group, i.e. the retirees' representation as moving away from his male social spheres.

Secondly, throughout the book I have explicitly emphasized the rigid division between the relative spheres of men and women. For example, the home as a domain controlled by women, and the clubs as strongholds of male working culture. This was, indeed, dramatically exemplified in the women's celebration. The intention of *'tekin' the club'* displayed a recognition that this area of social life (club life) is normally controlled by men. Moreover, the obscene behaviour, as well as forming part of a celebration of women's sexuality, can also be interpreted as an act of protest or rebellion, albeit impotent, against male control. It is important to emphasize the significance of the gender differentiation in relation to the man's retirement celebration. Despite the connection between women's power and the man's social withdrawal and isolation, the connection should not be seen as a result of the pressure of women. The image of the pressurizing and sexually dominant woman stands as a cultural representation of men's potential isolation only in that it symbolizes a withdrawal to home life; a movement into a female controlled domain.

WOMEN

It is difficult to speculate about the degree to which women can be said to have been marginalized with respect to cross-generational contexts of socializing as a result of ideological and structural changes, and the diminished significance of women's community roles (3). Amongst peers, at least, the ability to maintain contact is considerably greater than is the case for elderly men. Their social arenas are more convenient, such that problems of mobility represent a lesser threat. Their informality and their independence from the waged labour market make them resistant to the kinds of changes which have revolutionized the nature of the working men's clubs such that the number of old style all-male clubs are becoming fewer. Thirdly, particularly in the case of those clubs for the elderly which are predominantly used by women, a certain resilience stems from women's superior organizational qualities (built up through organizational responsibilities which were implicit in some of the various community roles which many women held) and their long established contact with the agencies which sponsor the clubs. Lastly, of course it should not be forgotten that in old age there are, in comparison to men, more women that can be kept in touch with. The social networks are not so abruptly threatened by the loss of members through death.

Despite the greater ability to maintain contact, this sexual disparity is itself double edged. In the clubs where there was a male presence it was clear that the death of male members was viewed with a greater sense of loss. Similarly, whilst new female members were politely introduced to the clubs, a greater fuss was made about the new men. This is perhaps not surprising, given this demographic disparity and the problems the clubs had in attracting men generally, but it is still necessary to account for why this disparity should be problematic in itself. It may be, in a general sense, that the presence of men is analogous to the presence of members of the family, i.e. they are the symbol of the successful execution of women's supportive domestic role. Indeed, the ability to create the right ambience for men was often unambiguously cited as a necessary and positive club quality. This presence may also be seen as indicative of the continuity of women's sexual value. However, I feel that desire for reduction of the disparity is quite simply an expression of an awareness of their marginality as a social group which is negatively labelled within the wider social context. Women appeared acutely aware of this in negative reference to the elderly group containing a gender dimension (i.e. as opposed to merely the connotations of institutionalization). For example, in explaining explicitly that her club suffered from a lack of men, one woman told me that, *"when us women is all together it's like we're all a bunch of owld hags....noot better to dee than gossip.*" The implication is that the male to female disparity represents conditions under which women feel and experience internalized negative stereotypes to a greater degree.

CONCLUSION

I have argued that women's ability to maintain contact with their social networks in old age is considerably greater than it is for men. The threat of isolation for men is culturally represented as movement into a female domain. This explains the representation of retirement for men as threatening domination by women, and to an extent, the characterization of the arenas of male social networks as male strongholds. Conversely, in the case of women, old age is characterized as marginality for a negatively perceived social group. This has ramifications in these social groups respectively. Firstly, some conflict between men becomes characterized as a result of 'coming under the influence of the wife'. Secondly, in all-women social networks conflict arises out of a tension between the desire to maintain the consistency of the group and a desire to narrow the sexual disparity. These points will be developed in the next section on 'association and conflict'.

2-SOCIAL RELATIONS BETWEEN THE ELDERLY: ASSOCIATION AND CONFLICT

Simone De Beauvoir points to the image of serenity as the most prominent of all misconceptions about the elderly. She states,
'Clearly, there is one preconceived notion that must be set aside - the idea that old age brings serenity. It (mankind) has deliberately chosen to look upon the end of life as a time when all the conflicts that tear it apart are resolved.' (1970:539).

Echoing De Beauvoir's concern to challenge the stereotype of the serenity of the elderly the aim of this section is to show that, antagonism is a meaningful response to old age in this cultural context, and its form is linked to features of pre-retirement life. The exposition will be divided into two sections. The first will deal with male and female relations respectively, and the second will deal with antagonism in mixed gender contexts. I will outline a difference in the legitimacy accorded to conflict between men and women respectively, such that the social expectation of the elderly which De Beauvoir points is one demanded of elderly women to a greater extent than it is of men, and in the second part I will outline how the participants of the clubs for the elderly and specific aspects of the Club's organization and events, may or may not work in conjunction to minimize the potential of conflict, and promote the common association of members.

MALE AND FEMALE CONTEXTS

Following the exposition of the events in this first half of my discussion I argue, with other supporting data, that the form of such conflicting and antagonistic relations relates back to the experiences of pre-elderly years. In the case of men I stress the relationship between the organization and exigencies of mining, and conflict and antagonism. Reflecting the centres of women's roles, I stress the domestic sphere, family life, and community life. I then consider such antagonistic and conflicting relations in the context of the experiences of being elderly, and the transitions and ruptures involved in becoming elderly in this particular social context.

Instances of antagonism and conflict

WOMEN

(i) Doris, Hilda, Lilly, and Anne met once a week at the Ellington day centre. Doris and Lilly came from Widdrington where they were next door neighbours, Anne came from Ellington village, and Hilda came from Lynemouth. Before meeting in the club Anne had vaguely known Hilda whom she met in and around Ellington and at the local chapel on Sundays. Doris knew Hilda quite well because at one stage her daughter and

Hilda's son had planned to marry. Through being neighbours Doris and Lilly knew each other well and claimed that their neighbourly relationship, though not close, was a co-operative and happy one. Doris and Anne, Hilda and Lilly, and Lilly and Anne met for the first time in the centre between three and five years prior to my arrival. Hilda and Lilly were in their mid eighties, and Doris and Anne in their late seventies. All except Anne were widows.

Every week they sat together at the same table, talking and playing cards. Much of the conversation concerned Doris and Hilda's fairly antagonistic relationship. Lilly was involved in this, but Anne was clearly on the periphery. She usually just entered the conversation at a tangent with some information about her family. The others politely smiled or paid no attention to her, but Doris told me that the others were all sick of her stories which they interpreted as boasting. In the Doris-Hilda relationship Hilda was most vocally critical. She accused Doris of always moaning, of telling fibs and of unjustly saying bad things about the club helpers. Doris didn't usually respond to the criticism, but was quite depressed by it, and claimed she had done nothing to warrant it. Nevertheless, Lilly tried to defend her. On one occasion she played on Hilda's partial deafness. She explained to me that Hilda used to be a singer in a nightclub, and, gesturing to Hilda, who was playing a game of cards, she noddingly said. *"weren't you?"* Hilda automatically affirmed the gesture. Lilly used this to accuse her of fibbing. When Hilda replied that she hadn't heard her properly Doris took the opportunity to have a dig; *"are ee deef or wat woman, or has ya memory gone funny?"* Hilda protested that there was nothing wrong with her memory to which Doris replied, *"ee'd forget your own name if it wasn't written on your bracelet."* Hilda seemed quite hurt and protested to Lilly, *"are ee me friend or wat?"* Lilly replied that of course she was and the two women proceeded to hug each other. Hilda then explained to Doris that she meant no harm. She said, *"you're a canny lassie"* and explained that she wished that they could have been brought closer together by a marriage between the families. She said that she had been saddened that the marriage had been called off because Doris' daughter Eileen, *"was a lovely lassie.... wad have med a perfect daughter-in-law"*.

However, it was the marriage which appeared to underlie the antagonism. Hilda explained to me that her son had been broken hearted about the split with Eileen, and that the blame was to be put on Doris' shoulders; *"the bitch put the mockers on't and poisoned her off."* Nevertheless, she was largely relieved by the break because Eileen had proved to be unsuccessful in marriage. Her husband had left her because, *"shi's a rats tongue like her mother."* When I asked Hilda why she continued to sit with Doris, maintained the acquaintance, and hypocritically spoke highly of her daughter, she explained that, *"you nivver dee ney harm by givin' a kind word"*, and *"hatin' doesn't dee ney good....you divvent waz (piss) on your own doorstep."* Moreover, she wanted to stay friendly with Doris' friend Lilly who she spoke of very affectionately. When I asked Doris the same question she said, *"yuv got to keep the peace. Aa divvent want to seem like a bickering owld cat div Aa."*

Hilda and Doris' hot and cold relationship carried on unabated until Lilly left the club when she moved out of the area to live with her daughter in Newcastle. Suddenly, she became the object of criticism for a brief period. Doris accused her of *"dorty tricks"* and said she was an *"owld moaner"* who was always after sympathy for her various ailments. Hilda agreed and said that she had always been suspicious of her and thought her devious. They both agreed that she had served to stimulate tension between the two of them. As Hilda stated, *"shi was always rubbin' us two up together the wrang way"*. However, within weeks the usual antagonism resumed its normal course.

(ii) When I began work at the Hirst club there were three male members. Within a short time they had left. The first of these to leave had been sent down by the W.R.V.S. to keep the books. His officiousness was seized upon by the committee members who ostracised him, openly referring to him as *'Herr Commondant'*. The other men never became fully integrated into the club because an ambience and set of activities more conducive to women had been developed. Some women also left, complaining of cliquishness and suggesting that Flori, the club leader, had moulded the tone of the club and chosen the activities specifically in an attempt to engineer the men's departure and discourage further male participation.

One of the women who left, Hilda (the comedienne from the Oakville club), had been actively involved in the running of the club. She was Flori's next door neighbour. She claimed that she left the club because she was unhappy with the organization, but other participants told me that a row had been brewing between the two of them for a number of weeks.

On the night of the club's Christmas party Hilda turned up after an absence of almost two months. Flori said that she had no right to attend and accused her of only using the club on such occasions when she could gain from it. In this case she got a free meal. Hilda replied that it had been Flori who had abused the club by engineering the departure of the men and trying to make the club her own little private gathering. Flori said that the visitor was disgruntled only because she, *'the dorty old cow'*, couldn't bring her *'fancy man'* along any more. The argument then degenerated into a series of random insults, concerning their love lives and families, openly being shouted across the restaurant.

The events which occurred later in the evening, after the women had had a few drinks, stood in sharp contrast to the antagonism. The two women danced and sang together, hugged each other, and were partners in the kind of obscene play outlined earlier.

MEN

(i) I frequently used to drink with four men at the Linton and Woodhorn club. Bart was in his mid eighties, George and Jim were in their mid seventies and Dougie was in his mid sixties. All had been miners at Ashington pit, and for some time Bart and Jim had worked together in a team. Bart and Jim were good friends, but their relationship with the others was characterized by a degree of ambivalence. Dougie was a recent retiree who had left the pit with a sizeable redundancy package. All were married and lived with their wives, except Bart who had lived with his daughter since his wife had died.

When I first met the men they took an interest in my work and said that they had lots of interesting tales to recount about Ashington and their days at the pit, which would come out over a few beers. They agreed to let me use a tape recorder. Within little time they got used to this and they forgot about their assumed role as local historians. However, what came out of their normal bar room conversation was much more interesting. The following transcribed data gives an insight into the nature of their normally antagonistic relations. The transcription is edited to a degree since even after numerous listenings I find much of it imponderable. The interactions recorded took place over about ten minutes. The brevity only serves to indicate how antagonism is an integral part of male relations which requires little stimulation and time for development.

(When I arrived at the club the others were expecting George to arrive from the allotments and were talking about Jim's recent trip to Carlisle).

DOUGIE-"*Wey Aa divvent knaa how ya think ya caught the train from platform three. Am tellin' ya man it sans from platform fower."*

JIM-"*It waz platform three."*

BART-"*Divvent listen tuv him Dougie. He'd get a gliff if ya showed him back on ee's own hand. Aa bet ee doesn't even knaa wat time ee got the train."*

JIM-"*Are ee lot givin' us the heedgehog or wat? Anyway, here's George. Aa might get a bit of respect oot o' him. How gans it George?"*

GEORGE-"*Canny fettle, canny fettle."*

DOUGIE-"*Ha' ya been up at the allotments?"*

GEORGE-"*No....Aa've been up feeding the ponies."*

DOUGIE-"*How is it?"*

GEORGE-"*Clarty....mind ya, there's ownly two things worth having in the world....a dog and a horse."*

BART-"*Which wad ya pick if ya were on a desert island.... stranded like?"*

GEORGE-"*It wad ha' to be the horse. There's nout a horse cannat dee for a man."*

ANDY-"*Aa waddant want to try and have a meaningful and loving relationship with a horse."*

GEORGE-"*Wey that's fuckin' typical. Aall ee youngsters think aboot is sex afore everything else."*

JIM-"*Ya cannat blame him. We were all the sane. Aa waz

lang in gettin married, but Aa wazn't lang in mekin' up for it."

BART-"*Magnus Magnusson speaks.... give him a starter for ten. Wat div ee knaa aboot the meaning of love? Ya haven't seen your missus bar meal times for fifty yors.*"

JIM-"*Mebee, but loves ney question o' time.*" GEORGE-"*Ya divvent knaa wat ya taakin' aboot. Can ee tell us wat love is? It's summet o' the imagination....fairy stories.*"

JIM-"*Wey a hard faced owld bugger like ee wad have to say that. Aa knaa wat it is. Aa've felt it.*"

GEORGE-"*Aye....Aa'll gan get mesell a pint of it....howay man.*"

(The conversation proceeded for some time like this, gradually deteriorating into a series of insults. However, out of the antagonism, the only real expression of ambivalence about one of the participants came when George went to the toilet and Jim took the opportunity to tell me that he was untrustworthy and dishonest. When George returned from the toilet he picked up his coat to leave).

GEORGE-"*Aa'm off to find a better class of intellect for company. Afore Aa gan Aa've got one that'll settle yuz aall.*"

DOUGIE-"*Howay then brain o' Britain.*"

GEORGE-"*How many days are there in the yor?*"

(The others mulled over where the catch could possibly be before conceding that they couldn't find the answer).

GEORGE-"*Wey Aa bet yuz aall forgot the leap yor. There's three hundred and sixty five and a quarter of course.*"

(George promptly left the club).

JIM-"*Ee's a good marra, but ee's always tryin' to get one up on ya.....Aa divvent knaa why ee does it we're all mates alike in here.*"

BART-"*See if ya can lick this one. Ya knaa there's ney full moon ney more.*"

DOUGIE-"*Howay then. Aa'm gettin' chowked o' this.*"

BART-"*Wey there's been none since the astronauts took them samples o' moon rock.*" DOUGIE-"*Ya like a bunch o' fuckin' bairns ee lot. Aa get more fuckin' sense cot of the granbairns.*"

BART-"*Wats up wi your fettle Dougie. Are wi not good enough for ya now yuv got all this money?*"

DOUGIE-"*Haddaway and shite man. Aa cannat mek ney sense oot of ees lot.*"

(Dougie promptly finished his drink and left).

BART-"*Aa divvent knaa wats gettin' intuv ees heed. Ney doobt the money's summit to dey with it.*"

JIM-"*Aye....wat with ees 'time share leisure unit' in Estapona.*"

BART-"*Flash or wat. Ees missus'll be behind it an' aall. Packin' him off to Marks and Spencers and kittin' him oot in aall that sporty gear. Aye....women....they're aall the same. Keepin' up wi the Jones'. They'll be hoyin' cocktail parties under a marquee in ees back yard next.*"

JIM-"*Aye....ees just a pitman. Ees ney respect ney more for ees marras.*"

BART-"*Aye ya reit there.... Mind, ee can talk aboot*

respect. Where were ee in the strike."
    JIM-*"Ee knaa full well where Aa waz. Aa waz on the sick."*
    BART*"Very convenient....still drawin' ya packet though."*
    JIM-*"Aye man, Aa went home and took a hammer to me leg and got me wife to gouge me eye oot with a stick."*
    (The slander, insults, and antagonism continued until closing time when Jim and Bart left the club and walked home together).

The sources and significance of antagonism and conflict and the working life

MEN

The conversation displays an antagonistic element which is typical of male relations in this social context. The explanation of such relations is implicit, though only tenuously expressed, in local popular culture and the comments of people I worked with. These stress a link between the exigencies of pit work and male social relations. Writers have stressed a link between conflicting male relations and manual work such as mining. Rim-linger (1959:389-405) offers a functional physiological explanation, arguing that acts of aggression are normal outlets for the tensions and frustrations fostered by the physical and psychological

214

demands of pit work. Tolson (1977:58-80) points to a style of aggression emanating from the primary importance of physical attributes in working class males. The problem with these arguments lies in what they don't explain. Aggression is not the most prevalent distinguishing feature of the relations I have outlined. Rather, they are characterized by a combination of friendliness and antagonism. Antagonism is a hallmark of normal unproblematic relations. Such relations resemble Radcliffe-Brown's account of joking relationships (1952:90-116), which he describes as being characterized by 'permitted disrespect', where friendliness and antagonism are combined. Like in Radcliffe-Brown's characterization of the joking relationship, there is an obligation not to take offence. The transgression of such an obligation is explained and chastised by reference to the mores of male relations which are seen to have been inverted. As outlined earlier, these are specific to this working class mining context, and through their emphasis on egalitarianism, solidarity, equality, respect, honesty and trust, can be described as being characterized as a systematic homogeneity. When Dougie was seen to disrupt relations with his friends by aggressively responding to criticism and leaving the circle on a sour note of discord he was accused of monetary elitism, pretentiousness, and a lack of respect, i.e. the converse of such mores.

Where then can a link be found with the exigencies of the industry? For much of the history of mining the working process and structure of the industry involved the juxtaposition of individual economic pursuit and competition with mutual responsibility and co-operation. The pursuit of maximum productivity was stimulated by both economic gain and the enhancement of prestige and masculine self identity. The reckless pursuit of productivity threatened the others working on the seam. Restraint engendered by mutual responsibility was thus essential. Co-operation was also engendered in relation to the hierarchical employment structure within the pit (particularly before the unions became an effective force in industrial disputes).

The combination of friendliness and antagonism is not a direct reflection of these conditions. Rather, the potential for antagonism, which is endemic to these competitive conditions, is the inevitable test of the resilience of the necessary relations of co-operation and mutual responsibility. The resilience of these is seen as the difference between life and death.

This is a very precarious situation. There is a thin dividing line between antagonism for testing the resilience of relations and antagonism leading to real conflict and aggression. However, aggression is also seen as functional to the maintenance of below surface relations. As it was explained to me, it's better to deal with conflicts in a definitive manner on the surface, where they are of little danger, rather than on the coal face, where they can kill.

The normality of conflict in male relations is reflected

in a number of ways. An extreme reflection of this is the conscious citing of the ability to withstand conflict as the basis of friendship. In describing his friendship with Jim, Bart clearly implied this. This aspect of male relations is institutionalized and, indeed, celebrated in the procedures of the Buffs. Conflict is the very *raison d'etre* of the organization's existence, and its means of subsistence.

The premium placed upon the stability of male relations is also apparent. For the Buffs it is the breaking of club rules rather than any particularly severe moral transgressions which is brought to light in the formal airing of conflict between members and which provokes greater scorn and financial sanction. Conflict is then celebrated, but also maintained in specific boundaries, reflecting its inevitability but also its potential danger if not controlled.

WOMEN

Women also referred to material bases of conflict. It is seen as an inevitable consequence of living and working in small tightly-knit communities. As the organization of home and family life and participation in the various community roles were essentially the responsibilities of women, it is perhaps not surprising that these interrelated spheres are referred to in the explanation of conflict. This was strikingly exemplified by the comments of an elderly man I worked with. He told me that the old couple who lived next door constantly came to complain about the noise of his father's gramophone. They knew that it belonged to the man of the household, but even when his father answered the door to the old woman, she would always ask for the mother, and his father would always call her to give the apologies. The sources of conflict generated in these interrelated family-domestic/community spheres are numerous; disputes about space and noise infringement, and, as in the case of Hilda and Doris, inter-family love feuds, etc.

The data presents a fairly typical example of how relations between some women swing, often dramatically, between intense real conflict and friendship. Whereas in male relations antagonism is released through aggression or is symbiotic with friendship, the prevalent feature of women's antagonistic relations is an emphasis on resolution. In the case of Flori and Hilda the party represented a context for a cathartic confrontation and resolution of their dispute. In the case of Doris and Hilda the antagonism which had developed steadily throughout the term of the day centre, because of their underlying ambivalent feelings about one another was consciously, though only temporarily resolved by straight forward hypocrisy and hypocritical reference to a conveniently absent other.

Hilda's comments point to a basic reason for the necessity of conciliation. The comments invoke the symbolism of the household, i.e. the doorstep as liminal, an area of public and private, of community and individual. To fail to conciliate is, 'to piss on one's doorstep'; to offend and harm oneself as well as others. The symbolic root for the necessity of the maintenance of stable relations thus appears to be the stability of harmonious community life.

I must refer to an earlier argument to explain the perceived necessity of community harmony and the position of women in maintaining it. I have argued that women's supportive role is seen partially in terms of fostering the right physical and psychological conditions for the pitman to successfully, and safely fulfil his productive task. I have also argued that women's demands are represented as militating against the psychological well-being of the miner, that such demands inform controlling stereotypes which buttress the sexual division of labour, and that at a symbolic level the prevention of mining death is the imperative which legitimizes this division. This same implicit unspoken logic applies to the question of conflict. Women's participation in community roles served in the fostering of these desired conditions beyond the immediate domestic sphere. Conflict between women, which may stimulate disharmony beyond the immediate home, can be seen as similarly militating, and thus death threatening. Again, this imperative of the prevention of death is crucial. Just as it legitimizes the sexual division of labour, conversely it is the ultimate prohibition on antagonism between women. As this imperative gives greater force to the controlling stereotypes of women in their marital relationships (for example, the nagging wife), it also gives power to the stereotypes which serve to control women's conflict. Whilst men argue, women are, to quote Doris, "*bickering owld cats*".

Conflicting and antagonistic relations in relation to old age

MEN

Whilst the antagonistic dimension in the conversation between the elderly men that I have presented is rooted in pre-retirement, working experiences, it also relates to retirement, the ageing process, and the changing nature of the social category of the elderly. In specific respects the potential for antagonism in retirement is intensified. The status of the retiree is eroded.

Key ways in which status and masculine self identity may be undermined are through the loss of financial independence, loss of influence in relation to the working sphere, and the cessation of the competitive productivity of pit work itself. I noted earlier that specific activities can be characterized as effective responses to such erosion. Some such activities possess not only a productive, but also a competitive, element. The 'discussion' about love can be characterized as such. Discussion and persuasion were irrelevant. It degenerated into a series of random insults and the posing of unanswerable questions which performed the function of social control, ensuring that nobody could actually take part in what was left of the debate, and guaranteeing personal victory.

It is nonetheless insufficient to characterize such verbal competition as a kind of status compensatory activity. The extent to which the elderly men may refer to physical criteria as a source of masculine evaluation is undermined in old age. Much of the content of the conversation displays a clear and typical emphasis on knowledge and intellect; for example, the questioning of Jim's memory and overt references to intellect and 'brains'. I suggest this is indicative of an added significance knowledge and intellect attain through physiological ageing,

It is also important to reemphasize that the elderly have become an increasingly heterogeneous social category. The data I have outlined displays how specific aspects of this heterogeneity may represent new sources of antagonism. For example, much of the antagonism directed towards Dougie, the younger financial beneficiary of the new sizeable redundancy packages, can be seen to represent protest about the wealth which the older men have missed out on.

It is clear that these new sources of antagonism and the increasing heterogeneity of the elderly as a social category represent specific threats to the stability of the social relations of elderly men. Relations are further weakened by the fact that retirement involves the deprivation of the material bases for solidarity and co-operation provided by the exigencies of pit work. This threat is expressed in the cultural representation of retirement as a movement from the masculine spheres of work into the female domain of the home, so that the retiree comes under the greater influence of women. When Dougie broke from the group because of tiredness with the competitive form of conversation, the other participants made explicit reference to his wife without any background information or knowledge of the woman. At one level she was used as a vehicle to protest about his wealth. At another level his wife's influence was explicitly stated as a cause of his contravention of the mores of male relations.

Much of the conversation represents response to these threats. The baiting of one another and the unrelenting flow of petty insults represent a testing of relations. A similar response is the excessive restatement of the mores of male relations. The men continually demanded respect and reminded themselves that Dougie was *"just a pitman"*. The excessive restatement of the mores of male relations is most dramatically emphasized in the organization of the Buffs. Official club rules sanction behaviour which in most contexts would be considered normal. However, the elderly leaders made a point of interpreting and enforcing rules more literally and rigidly than designed. For example, the national leader of the organization, 'The Worthy Grand Primo', states that, 'brothers will be honest amongst brothers' (Payne. 1969: 1976). The phrase was constantly repeated and interpreted literally such that white lies and lies told for the purpose of fun were not tolerated.

Finally, the excessive restatement of mores is at the root of the commonly cited stereotype of the pedantry of the elderly, ridiculed by younger generations. The Buffs is just one arena in which this ridicule is acted out. Misdemeanours and rule transgressions were punished by a small fine which had to be thrown across the room into a box at the foot of the leader's table. The younger men who visited from time to time went out of their way to tell the most ridiculous lies. When ordered to pay a fine they made a point of missing the box and showering the leaders and the man who had to pick up the money from the floor with small change. Others would then accuse them of the intention to hit the leaders, to which the accused would reply, "*who....me....never!*" This would be declared a lie and the process continued. The event was not an occasion for permitted disrespect, nor an inversion of relations of status, which in the context of the Buffs, with its hierarchical structure of posts according to seniority, is dependent upon age. Indeed, many of the older men were clearly annoyed by this practice. It was permitted precisely because the funds the young men brought were essential. The elderly men were compliant in an act of their own humiliation. Their need for the charity of the young and their rigid adherence to rules were the focus of their ridicule.

WOMEN

The potential for antagonistic relations between women to be minimized by old age does not appear to be evident. Competition between women based on, for example, supportive roles within the family, continue to provoke antagonism. This was apparent in the others annoyance at Anne's family monologues which were interpreted as her boasting her skills as a mother and wife. Similarly, a number of club leaders refused to allow club open days where family members could visit. The leader told me these were always events of considerable tension and antagonism as women, "*show-off to the poor darlings who haven't got anybody*".

Antagonism has an added significance in old age. The heterogeneity of the elderly as a social category and physiological ageing have as much significance as sources of new antagonisms and as threats to social relations to women as they do to men. What is evident from the data is that negative stereotypes of the elderly are used within this antagonism. For example, in criticism, the women in the first passage frequently evoked the image of the physical decrepitude of their antagonist, and in the second passage, Flori evoked the image of the deviant sexual identity of the elderly woman. Moreover, whilst I have argued that controlling stereotypes of women may ultimately serve to control conflict, paradoxically, in specific circumstances such stereotypes also stimulate conflict. In the section on isolation and marginality I implied that specific contexts, particularly all female contexts, represent conditions under which women feel and experience internalized negative stereotypes to a greater degree. It was perhaps this kind of awareness which stimulated an interest among some of the members to maintain and encourage a male presence. This interest was the source of disagreement with the others who wished to keep the group all female, as it was prior to becoming an official club.

Conclusions

Men and women appealed to the material conditions faced throughout their lives as sources of antagonism, but the ultimate referent of the exigencies of pit work serves, on the one hand to explain and legitimize antagonism between men, and on the other hand serves as the ultimate prohibition on antagonism between women. The results are an emphasis on the resolution of conflict between women, and the treatment of conflict between men as a normal and, to an extent, a necessary feature of their relations. The ultimate expression of the latter is the institutionalization and celebration of such conflict in specific contexts, which also serve to emphasize boundaries within which it should be confined, such that male relations are not threatened with breakdown. In the case of women a series of controlling stereotypes serve to control such conflict. The evidence contradicts the stereotype of the serenity of the elderly. Antagonism attains an added significance and, potentially, an added power in old age, and the resultant tensions represent new threats to social relations.

MIXED GENDER CONTEXTS

> *'Here we are again,*
> *Happy as can be,*
> *All good friends,*
> *And jolly good company.'*
> *'Just like Darby and Joan,*
> *In a world of our own,*
> *We'll build a nest way in the west,*
> *Be it so humble we'll never grumble.*
> *Though the grey locks are showing,*
> *And the dark clouds are drawing,*
> *Fear won't betide us,*
> *Our love will guide us,*
> *Just like Darby and Joan.'*

The short songs which heralded the beginning of the club meetings expressed an intention of harmony and comradeship of the elderly participants. However, in reality, antagonism between members was a constant feature of club ambience.

The ambience in the Ellington Darby and Joan club appeared relatively harmonious. There was almost no overt antagonism, and on occasions where one may have expected conflict, for example when there were conflicts of interest over the nature of club events and its organization, differences were disguised with humour, and debates conducted cordially. Nevertheless, it was clear that there was a degree of hidden but latent antagonism. This was evident in the difference between the public faces of members and their private selves that I discovered in one-to-one interviews outside the club. Model club members who were never involved in any form of dispute and who socialized freely with all the members were often bitterly critical of the other participants.

In contradistinction to the appearance of harmony in the Ellington club the most striking feature of the Northumberland Close club was its openly antagonistic ambience. Outbreaks of open conflict were a constant feature of the club. On such occasions critical comments and accusations were openly passed between members over the length of the hall. Much of the conflict appeared to concern concrete issues, centring upon differing ideas about club organization or a concern with conduct. For example, members were criticized for talking whilst the leader was speaking, or were accused of attempting to swindle the club by making false calls in the bingo games.

However, it was clear that these supposed concrete concerns were usually just a vehicle for personal criticism and slander. For example, on one occasion when the members were discussing a proposed shopping trip one man suggested that a restriction should be placed upon the amount of money people could take. His reason was that on the previous shopping outing space on the return leg of the bus trip had been hard to find as other members, whom he mentioned by name, had filled the coach with their purchases. The suggestion was merely a way of mocking other members who were perceived to have attempted to have displayed their wealth. Most such criticism and slander was random, unstructured and openly insulting.

The antagonism which was publicly manifest in the latter context and privately expressed in the former was substantially similar. The sources of differentiation outlined earlier in the book are undoubtedly significant in relation to the antagonism within the clubs. Criticism and slander referred to class, income and occupational status (for example, accusations of snobbery and elitism, etc.), local community differences (derogatory references to others as coming from specific other communities invoke negative connotations which are instantly understood), and in-class classifications concerning politics (for example, the term 'scab'), ethnicity (for example, people of Italian origin were put down with comments like 'it's the Mediterranean mentality again'), and perceptions of the domestic lives of women participants (for example, as one woman informed us, "*Aa divvent knaa how Irene Kirkbride can expect to tell wuz how to run the club. Shi cannot even run her own home*").

This fact is perhaps inevitable given the uniqueness of these clubs in relation to other leisure organizations in terms of their containing a widely differentiated social mix. In specific instances the antagonism directly related to these sources of differentiation. For example class differences exist with respect to the organization of leisure. In the Northumberland Close club heated debates about differing ideas of organization at this level were a major terrain of conflict. Moreover, there was certainly a simmering resentment amongst a few of the members in the Northumberland Close club that the 'high class' enclave that their area used to be had been undermined by the inhabitants of the newer lower quality accommodation, many of whom attended the club.

However, just as most of the criticism and slander was random, the invocation of language reflecting these sources of differentiation was usually contradictory. This will become evident in what follows. Moreover, these sources of differentiation cannot explain why antagonism was an overt feature of the Northumberland Close club, but remained latent at Ellington. The social mix in the latter context was, in many respects, as varied as in the former. There were substantial differences in terms of the wealth of participants, their ages, and their communities of origin, and, as pointed out earlier, some such categories of differentiation are largely subjectively constructed (i.e those based on day to day living in the home and in the family sphere) and, thus, I would suggest, are endemic to most contexts in the area. The point of this subsection of the book is to show in which way these sources of differentiation are significant in relation to the expression of antagonism, and, more importantly to explain why antagonism was an overt feature of one of the contexts discussed, but remained a mere potentiality in the other.

The language of sources of differentiation in the expression of fundamental antagonisms

I noted in the section on roles and status that participants were often concerned not only to distance themselves from the elderly group, but also within the elderly group. Being within the group perhaps implies an awareness of conformity to one's own negatively stereotypical images of the elderly. Distancing implies the definition of self in contradistinction to the other elderly. This was done in a number of ways, but of crucial significance here is participation in the club under the auspices of an organizer/helper role as opposed to an ordinary participant/ user role.

In the Ellington club all members were allowed to adopt specific active roles (bingo caller, tea server, concert party member, raffle ticket seller, etc.) within the club, thus minimizing the potential of an organizer/helper to ordinary participant/user divide. In contradistinction to this its leader established a rigid division of labour in the Northumberland Close club where a group of fifteen members only, most of whom were her friends or fellow officials from the W.R.V.S., took responsibility for all the tasks. The situation mirrored that in the Ellington day centre which was unsuccessfully imposed by the Age Concern workers, except in this case the organizer/helper to ordinary participant/user divide was between members only rather than between members and younger volunteers. However it was offensive at the same levels, i.e. it involved the limitation of access to participation in the various tasks which are central means of maintaining personal value in these contexts.

The result of this was clear to see in the comments of members who left the club. People left complaining that the club was for the '*aad aad*', and that it felt more like a rest home than a Darby and Joan, pointing in verification of this to the fact that some of the participants were wheelchair bound, and residents of the local sheltered home for the infirm elderly. However, there were as many wheelchair bound and semi-institutionalized participants in the Ellington club, but no such complaints were aired.

The point is that the organizer/helper to ordinary participant/user divide was seen as representing a cared to/cared for divide, where this limitation of access was seen to have ground the excluded participants down to the status of those against whom they wished to differentiate themselves, i.e. the disabled, semi-institutionalized and essentially dying. Such differentiation was subjectively possible for all the membership in the Ellington club, but generally speaking, since all members, including the disabled, were allowed to actively participate in the execution of club tasks to an extent of their own choices, a carer to cared-for divide was not an issue.

Amongst those who remained in the Northumberland Close club a considerable cleavage developed between the general membership and the organizer/helpers (Mrs Pratt's inner 'circle'). Though this limitation of access was a prevalent source of discontent amongst the former group of members it was rarely openly expressed within club discussions or in instances of conflict. The subject was perhaps taboo, particularly given the presence amongst their ranks of the disabled and semi-institutionalized.

Rather, hostility towards the organizer/helper group was couched in terms of an identification of exaggerated elitism. This identification of the group was exaggerated in the concrete debates about club organization. For example on one occasion the leader organized a lavish buffet dinner which was paid for by the W.R.V.S. One of the members complained that a more modest pea and pie supper would have sufficed. When one of the leader's group pointed out that the dinner had been paid for by the W.R.V.S. rather than from club funds, and that members should have been grateful that she had managed to extract so much money from the umbrella organization, another participant mockingly derided her rationale by claiming that the meal was intended to show other clubs in the area that the Northumberland Close club aimed to cater for 'a better class of people'. Two members from the leader's group became foci of ridicule; a woman who had been the headmistress at a local school, and her male companion who was from one of the Italian families and had been a wealthy hotel and cafe owner in the area. Participants mimicked the haughty laughter of the former, joked about the decadent attire of the latter and exaggeratingly mimicked his swaggering style of walking. The group as a whole were labelled as elitist. They were referred to mockingly as the 'hobnobs', the 'Windsors', or the 'Bellamy's' (an aristocratic family portrayed in a television soap opera). The language in which the antagonism towards this group was couched can be seen to originate in the sources of differentiation outlined, i.e. notions of elitism may stem from perceptions of class, occupational and income differences. However, this example shows the contradictory use of this language, since the members of the respective groups were in no way divided along lines of class, occupation, or income. Rather, aspects of the activities and suggestions of the organizer/helper group and the characteristics of its members (i.e. those who could be seen to most visibly exemplify the label of elitism), were selectively chosen and exaggerated to construct a hostile identity of elitism.

The construction of the label of elitism was used to convey the real and offensive division which existed in terms of the access to participation in the various club tasks, which could not be concretely expressed. Thus the significance of these sources of differentiation is that they may be exaggeratedly used to generate discourses through which more fundamental, though often unutterable, sources of antagonism are expressed.

Levelling and the construction of a bond of association

Despite arguing that the significance of these sources of differentiation stems from their providing the language in which more fundamental sources of antagonism are couched, the minimization of consciousness of these differences as they exist between participants is nevertheless important if fundamental antagonisms are to be deprived of their means of expression. A series of conscious and unconscious processes in the clubs for the elderly serve in the minimization of the significance of differentiation between members. In developing this argument I will draw directly on the work of Victor Turner.

Starting from the work of Van Gennep who argued that rites of passage involve the three distinct phases of 'separation', 'margin (or limen)', and 'aggregation', Turner developed the notion of communitas (Turner.1969). The fundamental point of his argument is that in the marginal or liminal phase the condition and social relations faced by the initiate are characterized by their lack of structure and differentiation as opposed to the structure, differentiation, and hierarchy which characterize the states from which and into which the initiate passes. The notion communitas refers to these undifferentiated social relations and the existence of a 'generic human bond' between initiates. In discussing this idea in the context of modern industrial society he states:

'What appears to have happened is that with the increasing specialisation of culture, with progressive complexity in the social division of labour, what was in tribal society principally a set of transitional qualities "betwixt and between" defined states of culture, and society has become itself an institution of the centralised state.' (1969:107)

The institutionalization of liminality is evident in a number of contexts. One category of such contexts is Goffman's 'total institutions' (1961). An essential characteristic of total institutions is 'the stripping and levelling process which.... directly cuts across the various social distinctions with which the recruits enter' (Turner's emphasis).

Within the clubs for the elderly, processes served to work against differences amongst the membership. These were instigated at the levels of general membership and club organization. Firstly, though not total institutions, the specific clubs for the elderly displayed a similar. 'stripping and levelling' process, which served to foster a perception of equality between members. Secondly, differences were transcended by the construction of a 'common bond of fellowship.'

The ability to instigate these processes in the Ellington club explains why antagonism remained only as a potentiality. The inability to instigate these processes and, indeed the organization of events which were directly contrary to these processes provide further reasons why differences between the membership were made more apparent and ultimately played a part in sowing the seeds of overt antagonism in the Northumberland Close club.

(i) Levelling-(a) Levelling amongst the general membership: Such a levelling was an implicit part of the conversational preoccupation with critique of the young which I discussed earlier. For example, participants who accused others in the clubs of elitism, snobbery, poor home management and so on, in the privacy of an interview or in whispered comments within the club, rarely voiced them openly in this context, but were often conversationally preoccupied with directing similar critiques at the young of the area. I think that it is feasible to argue that the potential for differences between members to become apparent was actively minimized by their deflecting the expression of their ambivalent and critical feelings about one another toward an absent and abstract younger generation.

(b) Levelling as a feature of organization: The basis for the minimization of difference was built upon and militated against in the Ellington and Northumberland Close clubs respectively. This can be shown by considering how the similar events and features of the clubs were organized differently. Each week members of both clubs were expected to bring items (usually food) to the club which could be given away in an 'everyone wins a prize' draw. At the Northumberland Close club, when particularly lavish and expensive items (for example, joints of meat, turkeys, large cakes, etc.) were given, the chairwoman announced this fact and asked the membership to applaud the gift giver for his/her generosity. All the items were then openly displayed for the winners to be able to choose their prize. By contrast, the members at Ellington handed their gifts to the prize draw organizers who promptly put them into paper bags to conceal them, and then privately thanked each gift giver. Then as each member's ticket number was called they won the right to a 'lucky dip'.

There were similar differences between the clubs in the organisation of trips and holidays. Though inexpensive, those organized by the Northumberland Close club were beyond the prices which some members could afford. At Ellington no outing was organized unless it could be paid for almost completely from club funds, even though this meant that these had to be modest events.

Perhaps most significantly, considerable differences existed at the level of democratization in club organization. Both club leaders attempted to make all major club decisions democratic, but where clear conflicts of interest arose, the Northumberland Close leader almost always vocally intervened and on occasions imposed decisions which favoured the interests of a group of members. The resentment which this caused was further exacerbated by what some members considered to be an authoritarian style of leadership. Officials wore W.R.V.S. uniforms and sat at desks at the front of the hall facing the members. Conversely, the Ellington Club leader sat amongst the members and in almost all respects she gave the appearance of being an ordinary member. Moreover, she appeared to distance herself from direct decision making, but where no resolution could be achieved she skilfully enforced resolutions. She intervened and brought debates about club organization to an unresolved end by announcing the necessity of club events to proceed. Then outside of the club she would make a concrete decision. On occasions such decisions were given the appearance of anonymously developing over time, or she would announce that she had had to impose a decision because of the impossibility of the other alternatives that had been discussed, about which she was often lying. On a number of occasions she used a method she was well practiced in; the exploitation of the perception of her weaknesses. She often claimed that she had made decisions, after having forgotten members' objections.

(c) Conclusions: In certain crucial respects the Northumberland Close club failed to instigate the type of institutionalized levelling process which was largely achieved in the Ellington club. The organization of the prize draw provided members with a means of gaining esteem in the club according to their spending power. Secondly, it allowed a system of redistribution to develop, where some members made a point of picking cheaper items and allowing the better prizes to be passed on to others who, *'hev a need of it'*. Many of the members considered the practice highly patronising, arguing that they had no intention of attending the club to be recipients of charity. (The giving of food is the most basic form of charity). The organization of this event, and the costing of events such as trips, which led to the exclusion of poorer members from participation, served to, heighten the visibility of differences (particularly of wealth) between members and, provide the means by which this visibility could be further exacerbated by members themselves. Conversely, in the Ellington club the organization of events at a cost affordable to all, and the preservation of anonymity in the organization of the prize draw served to conceal such differences between members. Finally, whilst the chairwoman of the Ellington club fostered an equality of power accorded to competing interests amongst the membership, the authoritarian appearance of decision making in the Northumberland Close club served to heighten resentment and division based on suspicions that power was being unfairly accorded to specific interests in the club.

(ii) A common bond of fellowship:(a)Introduction-Earlier in the book I argued that the elderly people I worked with hold a picture of community which has been, objectively, eroded and deprived of its material referents, an image that is essentially mythological. However, the maintenance of this picture does not involve a blanket denial of facts. They recognize this erosion and specific mythological aspects in their descriptions. Thus, I argued that this portrayal of community is not explainable as a denial of facts, but rather as an unconscious or symbolic intentionality, i.e. it serves specific purposes. One of these purposes concerns the problem of membership differences. The point is to emphasize that community is a state of mind, an awareness among a group of people that, as Cohen states,

'the members of a group have something in common with each other, which distinguishes them in a significant way from the members of putative groups.' (1985:12).

The construction of this picture of community serves the purpose of promoting a commonality between club members. The conversation and entertainment within the clubs, which were predominantly concerned with the celebration of this mythologized community, and other specific aspects of club organization, served to sanitize differences, symbolically reconstitute a central virtue by which this community is characterized, i.e. its co-operative nature, in the club context, and stimulate a discourse of commonality of experience.

Up to now I have implied that, as a consequence of the process of levelling, association between the members of the clubs, to the extent that it existed, was by a perception of equality, where differentiation is minimized. However, differentiation was not totally denied. Rather, the celebration of community and club organization (i.e. the sanitizing of difference, etc.) together serve to form a common bond of fellowship.

This mirrors Turner's notion of a 'generic human bond', but rather than suggesting an automatic communitas of the elderly I am emphasizing the construction of a human bond which if established has the potential to transcend differences, rather than being indicative of their non-existence.

(b) The discourse of commonality: As I showed earlier in the book the main characteristics of both conversation and entertainment was that they were firmly local and concerned with the past. These spatial and temporal aspects of discourse within the clubs played an integral part in the common association of club members.

A central aspect of the discourse was the critical polarization of community and outside. The inwardly concentric nature of this discourse established a means of common bond between members as northerners, as inhabitants of a small cluster of mining communities (i.e. the Ashington area), and as inhabitants of smaller communities with unique characteristics. The latter was the closest achievable means of marking off members of specific clubs as being unique. The implication here is that the more inward and specific such identifications become, the stronger the sense of a bond of common identity between members will be.

The overriding concern with the past, both in historical critical contrast, and in sessions of collective reminiscence cannot be seen as simple nostalgia. The concern is with a community apparently of the past which was essentially 'theirs', i.e. they were the members of this community, and though it has been substantially eroded, they are still the guardians of its values, and the survivors of its era. This in itself is a fundamental basis of association between the elderly participants, but also of importance is the fact that this community provides a model for harmonious relations within the clubs since its outstanding feature is that of co-operation. Co-operative relations are fostered at other levels of club organization.

(c) Reconstitution of co-operative relations: Perhaps the most important institutionalized expression of comradeship between members which was practiced in all clubs was the way in which the absence, sickness, or bereavement of members was dealt with. Immediately after the introductory song, announcements were made about such members, and get well soon or condolence cards were signed by everyone present. Informally, a series of expectations existed for all the club members. They were expected to keep the club informed about both the condition of those who were sick or those who had recently lost a spouse, and about the help and attention they were receiving. Moreover, when members were unaccountably absent, friends or neighbours from within the club were expected to make enquiries about the reasons for their absence and to report back to the club with information. Whilst illness and bereavement within the local area and amongst relatives generally was discussed, their primary concern was with club members.

Whilst this practice embodied a series of active responses, i.e. the sending of cards, the enquiries, and the provision of information, members were never pressurized to do more. The severity of complaints made about the N.H.S., Social Services, and the families of the sick or bereaved indicated clearly that it was these agencies which were seen to hold the responsibility for active care (however, as I will show in the following section on, 'responses to the physiological realities' of ageing, complaints made about the former of these are indicative of a scepticism which, ultimately, informs a principle of self help). This club response to absence, sickness or bereavement was, then, merely an expression of concern. It was impotent as an expression of care. In this sense it represented, I would argue, a microcosmic symbolic counterpart of the perceived social relations of the mythologized community; a reconstruction of co-operative relations, whose primary function was as a basis of association between members.

(d) Sanitizing difference: I argued earlier that the critical contrasting, or exaggerated polarization of past and present, and a sanitizing humour served in the idealization of the past, the characteristics of 'their' generation, and the ideals implicit in the notion of community that is celebrated in the clubs for the elderly. This is of importance in this context, for it involved the portrayal of images of harmony and comradeship, and served to submerge potential contradictions to the ideal by underplaying and representing in a humorous light social differences and past conflicts. This provides, I would argue, a further essential basis for harmonious relations in the present club context.

(e) Differences between the two contexts: As shown extensively earlier in the book, mining is central to the image of this mythological community, which in itself is central to the process of constructing a bond of association. This is the key to understanding the differences between the two contexts in the extent to which antagonism was evident. I showed that people often recognized the centrality of mining to the structure of the community and ultimately their indirect or direct former dependence on it. However, I also showed that people distanced themselves in terms of occupational group cultural characteristics. Identification with mining which was, on the whole, common to members of the Ellington club, did not occur in the Northumberland Close club, since the majority of the participants were from non-mining backgrounds. Thus, unlike the Ellington club, in the Northumberland Close club there was a significant cleavage in the extent to which participants could engage in discussion of shared history, or in other words a commonality of experience. Moreover, the images of community celebrated by the mining people, and implicit in the forms of popular 'culture' performed by the entertainers, were largely inappropriate, in that whilst non-mining people could understand these images, they could not directly relate to them. Indeed, they were often images to be ridiculed rather than celebrated and cherished.

Conclusions

Clearly, the social differentiation of pre-retirement years persists into old age. In social contexts of the elderly such differentiation is often manifest in either overt or covert antagonism and differences of interest between participants. However, its primary relevance in relation to the question of antagonism is in the sense that the language of such differences is used to convey a more fundamental antagonism which relates to the ageing process. I have found that the extent to which such differentiation is evident may be minimized by, for example, participants' use of an absent younger generation to deflect potential criticism between peers. This is the beginning of what I have called a process of 'levelling'. However, in these contexts its success is largely dependent on the extent to which institutionalized aspects of club life (styles of leadership, organization and costing of events, etc.) serve to minimize and conceal membership differences. This may also be accompanied by what I have described as a 'common bond of fellowship'. Its significance is in the transcendence rather than the concealment of differences. Its central feature is a notion of community of which participants are the members. It is celebrated and reconstituted through conversation, entertainment, and club practices. It serves as a focus for commonality, or common identification, and as a model and image of harmonious relations. The mining experience is central to this notion of community and, thus, to the construction of this bond. As such, such a bond cannot be made where there is a significant cleavage between mining people and non-mining people. This is more than an occupational divide. It is, in essence, a cultural divide, where the mining experience is wholly inappropriate to non-mining people as a medium of association.

3-RESPONSES TO THE PHYSIOLOGICAL REALITIES

Generally speaking, the major dangers of the physical and mental decline which characterizes the ageing process are perceived to be those of depression and apathy, induced, for example, by illness, either, bringing about discontinuity in the momentum of life, directly disabling participation in activities, or bringing home the fear that activity will result in further illness or death. This sub-section of the book is an attempt to outline the elderly people's perceptions of these aspects (i.e. physical and mental decline) of the ageing process. I will outline a series of informally or formally expressed principles and notions which concern how physical and mental decline should be perceived and positively responded to. I will show the bases upon which these are constructed, show how they are celebrated and reinforced in social contexts of the elderly, outline how they are constructed in interplay between individuals and social contexts, and show how contravention of such principles is discouraged. The fact that these are, in part, responses to the dangers of depression and apathy should become evident.

Acceptance

Instances of illness are commonly perceived and accepted as indications of ongoing and inevitable physical decline in old age rather than isolated events. A statement which is presented as a conclusive explanation of illness, *'it's just owld age'*, conveys this inevitability. Its constant repetition is such as to constitute part of a common stock of vocabulary, its, meaning is totally unambiguous and instantly understood, and its validity is rarely questioned.

Acceptance is also a commonly held principle around which life in old age should be guided. Actions interpreted as contravening this principle become the subjects of ridicule and criticism. The way in which the remarriage of peers was discussed exemplifies this point.

A couple, both of whom were in their late seventies, who had met in the Ellington club, announced their intention to marry. Derisory comments implied that the woman was futilely engaging in the assertion of a false youthfulness. One woman stated, *"what she thinks she's proving I'll nivver knaa....she's no spring chicken....silly owld woman.... on her way oot like the rest of wuz"*. Other remarks concerned the practical aspects of the remarriage: *"A divvent think it's right....a risk like....at her age...wey she'll be a burden of him"*. This cautionary note was emphasised by a man who relayed the experience of an acquaintance. He explained that after the man's first wife had died, a woman who had also been widowed came to his home to cook and clean for him on a day to day basis. In order to make the relationship appear respectable the man decided, against the protestations of his family, to offer to marry the woman. She accepted and they began to live together. After some years the woman became progressively senile and bed bound and the roles which were envisaged at the beginning of the marriage were reversed, as he became domestic labourer and carer. The stress caused by this heavy work proved too much for this relatively fit and healthy man. This stress, it was argued, lay behind the sudden chest infection which caused his eventual death some two years before his wife died. It was also explained that the failure of the woman's family to more forcefully dissuade her from remarriage had been a source of tension between the two families for some time after the death of the man.

It is evident that the degree of legitimacy accorded to men's remarriage and that of women is considerably different. What is important in this context is that the remarriage of women, at least, is regarded as indicative of contravention of the principle of acceptance. It is ridiculed as a futile denial of the inevitability of physical decline in old age, cautioned against, and, as the data in the latter paragraph suggests, criticized by the invocation of a moral dimension. Marriage involves a series of commitments which may not be satisfactorily executed in old age, the consequences of which may be as severe as death. As such it is questionable whether remarriage should be entered into.

Confrontation through ridicule and humour

Self ridicule and/or humour is perhaps the most salient form in which the elderly people I worked with expressed the problems of physical and mental decline and the fact of the imminence of death. I shall turn to some examples of this.

i) Loss of memory and physical decrepitude: A woman commenting on the state of a friend's memory stated, "*the only way ee knaa your own house is by the number on the door*". Another woman commented on the matter of an appointment, "*give wuz a date two days afore the coach Bans and we might remember two days too late so we turn up on time*". A woman commenting on the disability and restricted mobility of participants in a club stated, "*You can tell when we're coming.... there's more clankin' of metal than tappin' of feet*". In one particularly severe case a woman answered every question asked where she needed to give an opinion with self ridiculing comments which explained that the state of her physical and mental retardation rendered her completely unable to make any sense or comment of worthwhile value. As a consequence she had become isolated in the Ellington day centre where she was a member, as she could not be relied upon for any meaningful conversation.

ii) Death: A man commenting on a proposed shopping outing organized by one of the clubs stated, *"Wey Aa'm not ganna buy me ticket now, Aa might be six foot under by the time the bus comes roond for wuz....what a waste of money"*. A woman delighted in telling me the following joke. A child was 'bublin' (crying) because his kitten had died. His mother told him not to worry because it would go up to heaven. Some time afterwards the child was found by his mother writing a letter. She asked him what he was doing, to which he replied, *"I'm writing a note to God to tell him how to look after Tiddles"*. She told him that there was no point in doing this because there was no post to heaven, to which he replied, *"It's all right I'll send it up with Grandma coz she's going soon"*. The leader of the Northumberland Close joked about a death which occurred on an over sixties club holiday in Spain she had recently returned from. All had gone well until the last week when poor Mr Nicholas took a sudden bad turn and died. His body was transported back to Ashington and opened for the relatives to see. They all agreed that his death was a terrible shame, but, referring to his sun tan, one of the relatives said that, *"he does look well, mind you!"* The same woman on a number of occasions referred to the club as *'the one foot in the grave club'*(4).

iii) Sex and death: A large degree of the content in conversation concerns sex. Frequently this is associated and juxtaposed to the issue of death. For example, one elderly woman stated, "*divvent get us worked up with aall this talk of love....Aa might just be tempted.... one more night of passion would finish us off Aa'd be sure*". Similarly, an elderly man stated in reference to the issue of the AIDS epidemic, "*It seems like us lot and the young'ns has a lot in common noowadays....one night of passion and we're liable to end up deed*".

iv) Age: Numerous comments made in the opening addresses of club leaders referred to the age of the participants. For example, "*I've got a birthday message here for a man of ninety five. It says, love Mam and Dad*". A man at the North Seaton club referred to it as the club for "*the aad, the grey, and the nattery*". The ridicule expresses a series of real problems encountered by the elderly, of a physical or psychological (i.e. physical decrepitude and loss of memory), existential (i.e. death), or socially constructed nature (for example, stereotypes of the elderly). The comments can then be read as a commentary on conditions faced by the elderly. Indeed, many of the comments cannot be read as self evidently humorous. Despite this fact the comments are almost always responded to with a degree of hilarity. This implicit expression of the realities of ageing in ridicule alongside the humour with which such ridicule is received was evident in the ambivalent reactions of a number of the participants. One woman commented that despite her laughter at another woman's remark about her poor memory she did in fact find these comments insulting and a source of friction between the two of them. Others expressed shock at the leader of the Northumberland Close club's comments about death. Another woman explained that, "*Aa had no idea until Aa came here that Aa waz such a good comedienne*". Thus, despite a humorous reception for such ridiculing comments, they are often received also as insulting or shocking or presented without the explicit intention of humour.

Of course, laughter often comes at points of ambivalence and unease, but what I want to stress here is that the expression of the problems of ageing through ridicule and humour is not in any way an inevitability or natural. Their conflation is learned through participation in the social networks of the elderly. The clubs for the elderly serve to augment this process through, for example, the encouragement of humour, presentation of the type of formal joking outlined, and plays where the problems of the elderly form the main source of humour. A play I saw at the North Seaton club and the response of the club participants to the play exemplifies the melding together of the expression of the problems of ageing with humour and ridicule. The play was about an old woman's shopping trip to the centre of the town. First she took the bus, but because of her arthritic legs she took a few minutes to get on. This caused considerable consternation on the part of a number of people trying to get to work on time. Then she called at the post office to get her pension only to find out that she was a day too early. Then she went Christmas shopping with some savings she had withdrawn and she managed to infuriate a group of customers who were waiting at the same till, as she took so long working out how much the goods were in pounds, shillings and pence. After this she went home causing considerable delays as she entered and left the bus. On returning home she castigated herself for her stupidity; she had bought all the necessary Christmas presents but had forgotten that it was still only July.

There are a number of points to be made about the play. Despite the fact that the play was largely stripped bare of most of the normal mechanisms which constitute a comedy, it was received with a high degree of hilarity. The hilarity stemmed from an exaggerated representation of the type of problems faced by many of the elderly spectator/participants (poor memory, poor physical mobility, etc.). It is plausible to argue that the extreme image of the retarded and decrepit old woman in the play was one against which the spectator/participants could distance themselves. Nevertheless, the difference between the woman in the play and many of the club participants was one only of degree. I would suggest that, in mocking the woman in the play in terms of problems which could be commonly related to, the play, in effect, mocked and ridiculed the elderly spectators in the club. Furthermore, it is not so much the exaggeration which explains the hilarious reception, since the spectators commonly recognize such problems as a source of humour. They are unambiguous signs. This contrast between the threadbare nature of the play and its imputed humour was expressed by a woman's ambivalent appraisal; "*It waz ney good, but it waz funny*".

Finally, it would be incorrect to imply that humorous self ridicule is fostered and learned exclusively in these social networks of the elderly. There is some pre-basis for this in the existence of a range of stereotypes and ridiculing humour about the elderly which the people I worked with draw upon. Secondly, the problems which elderly people face are particularly suitable subjects around which humour may be constructed. Within the wider society there are a series of fundamental issues which humour predominantly confronts. Notable among these are physical and mental abnormality, and death - hence, the plethora of jokes about the crippled and the mentally retarded. The amenability of the elderly as subjects of ridiculing humour lies partially in relation to this in that physical and mental retardation and their proximity to death are prevalent concerns in their lives. Thirdly, a pre-basis far self-ridiculing humour lies in a notion referred to within the community as 'corrida'. Corrida means the ability to make humour out of ones predicament. The ability to show corrida is widely admired, and people are positively referred to as 'real corridas'. One man who people referred to as 'Humpty-

Backed Jack' typical. Many of his poems and jokes had been transcribed and were passed around for use in the club, thus reminding and reemphasizing the value of corrida.

The power to 'age well': The strength of the aged and management of the ageing process.

Despite having noted the acceptance of the inevitability of physical decline and its confrontation through self ridicule and humour, participants explicitly stated that individuals must learn positively to manage the ageing process. As the term implies, in line with this perception of the inevitability of physical decline, ageing is to be managed rather than denied.

Management of ageing is widely viewed as a moral precept, for its rationale lies not only in the egoistic concerns of a 'richer and longer life', or the desire to avoid major lifestyle changes brought about through illness, or total institutionalization, but also in relation to others. The spectre of being a physical or emotional burden upon others and the awareness of the in-family conflict which this may cause as loyalties and responsibilities are tested over the question of care is a common topic of conversation.

The concern to manage ageing positively is evident in a preoccupation with instances of illness and related issues such as medical aids and the medical services. However, formal medical services are treated with a degree of suspicion and scepticism. For example, people were constantly critical of the National Health Service. Criticism is usually implicit rather than explicit. For example, one man commented, "*One time Aa went the doctor give us the same stuff for me sore leg as he'd given us for me rash. When Aa went the next time he asked us if me rash had stopped. So Aa says, 'aye, aboot three yors ago hinny'*". Despite the implicit nature of much of the criticism, the scepticism has its roots in the dominant socialist critique of the state, and perceptions of regional political favouritism as discussed earlier.

Perceptions of the inadequacy of the official agencies of care fuel the common idea that management of illness is largely the responsibility of the individual (this, again, highlights the extent to which the representations of community are idealized in that this involves an implicit recognition that, whilst the community can be represented as an alternative and autonomous infrastructure, providing care, it is in reality severely limited in this respect). This is explicit in the commonly cited notion of 'ageing well'. People spoke of 'good agers' and 'bad agers'. The classification does not describe the relative differences in the extent to which individuals have been affected by physical decline, but rather describes positive or negative responses on the part of individuals to the disabling conditions which the rigours of ageing may bring about. Whilst 'ageing well' implies living successfully with the inevitable rigours of ageing, in certain cases outlooks which constitute 'ageing well' are seen to have a positive effect upon the individuals physical and mental condition.

Here I will outline the bases upon which this notion is founded and constructed and will show how events within the context of the social networks of the elderly, and in the clubs particularly, serve to celebrate the perceived foundation of this notion, foster outlooks which constitute 'good ageing', and discourage responses which are seen to constitute 'bad ageing', such that these contexts, at least temporarily, foster a symbolic assumption of control, and mastery over, the rigours of ageing.

Implicit in this notion is the assumption that 'ageing well' is a question of choice; a question of adopting the right outlook on life. This choice is possible because, to use a commonly cited term, the individual possesses within his/her 'power' the ability to age well. This 'power' constitutes the basis upon which the notion of 'ageing well' is built. Either implicitly or explicitly, the comments by the elderly people I worked with expressed a belief that they possessed specific strengths which were peculiar to their generation. The nature of these is fourfold. They stem from, experience, social marginality, and their historical circumstances, or lastly, are strengths realized only as a consequence of physical and mental decline (which is partially the cause of this marginality). The strength of marginality and experience is the perceived ability to comment objectively and critically upon social relationships and the social milieu. Physical decline implies a liberation from the dangers and 'madnesses' caused by sexual urges and competition (5). For example, one elderly man referred to the toilets in the working men's club as the *"brag room....the cause of all the battles....us owld fellas hev nowt to brag aboot ney more thank God....that's wat keeps the peace"*. Secondly, physical and/ mental decline in old age is seen to bring about the realization of a transcendence of an essential self over mind and body. Lastly, strength deriving from historical circumstances is implicit in the common perception of 'this generation' of this area as having the background experiences which facilitate coping with the rigours of ageing. These last two points are most pertinent in this context, but before they can be developed I must exemplify how the strengths of the elderly are celebrated in at least one social context. The poems of Humpty-Backed Jack which are recited at the North Seaton club are pertinent in this context.

'Aa'm Jack the humpty- backed coal man, Folk think Aa'm not mentally strang, Aa shovel coals in for a livin', So mebbie they're reit , mebbie wrang.

Aa hevn't had varry much schoolin', Me sums used to drive teacher mad, But Aa knaa, if Aa'm paid just two pennies Instead o' three, Aa hey been had.

Aa mind once the widow, aad Keene,y Wad pay me wi' breed and plum jam, "But ye canna buy beer wi' that, hinny" Aa says, "Aa'm a fully grown man".

She whimpered, "Aa'm just a poor widow", But Aa knew that hor stockin' was full, 'Cos she lay iv'ry neit wi' strange bodies, Not me though, Aa'm not sic a fyul.

She still wadn't pay me ma money, So, before ye, not me, could coont ten, Aa climmed back into the bowly, And hoyed aall the coals oot agyen.

That larnt the aad besom a lesson, For the coals were scattered aall ower, And the man that refilled them, charged her, Not me three clarty pennies, but fower.

Aa shud hey mentioned this sooner, Aa've been tekin' fits aall me life ,And Aa think that that is the reason, Ne lass fancied bean' me wife.

Aa'm aad noo and iver se weary, The leit in me eyes' gettin' dull, And sumtimes Aa worry, and wunder, What's gan t' becum of me shul.

Aa'd like it set up as a heedstone, (When me ingine stops deed in its track), Wi' these simple words engraved on't, "To the mem'ry of humpty-backed Jack."
From, 'Humpty-Backed Jack' (Coombs.— —:8-10).

The autobiographical poem portrays Jack as a physical and mental oddity (i.e hunch-backed, epileptic, and of low intellect), who as a consequence is marginal to the community and, thus could not fulfil the normal expectation of marriage. Nevertheless, he possesses a sense of cunning, wisdom, and a mental agility which is used against those who attempt to exploit his perceived weaknesses. Discussion of Jack which preceded the poetry was nostalgic and humorous and took up the themes of him as an oddity, and as marginal, and developed the scope of his perceived attributes. He was cunning, shrewd, and, above all, a witty and critical observer of life in the community. The significance of the poetry readings in the context of the clubs for the elderly and the explanation of their popular reception lies, I would suggest, in the fact that the conditions faced by Jack closely resemble those of the elderly. Both, to an extent, are seen as physically weak and socially (and sexually) marginal. Though never cogently stated, I would suggest that it is the physical and mental conditions of Jack and his resultant marginality which are viewed as the bases of his perceived attributes. In this sense too the poetry mirrors the situation of the elderly. Sontag has pointed to the myriad of metaphors which surround different illnesses and conditions(1979). Old age is usually characterized as tantamount to weakness. I would suggest that the poetry reading performs the role of celebrating and reinforcing a metaphorical inversion; their physical and mental decline and resultant marginality, which may be seen as weaknesses, are in fact to be seen as sources of strength. To an extent this corresponds to Turner's account of the sacred attributes of the marginal and low status in his development of the notion of communitas (1969:109-110).

In fostering this inversion the elderly are subverting the descriptions of the elderly by younger generations. This is borne out in common characterizations of the carer-cared for relationship where elderly people live with their sons or, more usually, daughters. People pointed to ambiguity over the definition of roles, emphasizing their roles as carers rather than the cared for. Others legitimized their presence in the home of their family in terms of their appeasing the fears of that family, such that in some cases they viewed themselves as either, unnecessarily adopting, or maintaining the pretence of, the cared for role. One man pointed to the constraining effects of such a situation when he told me that he had had to cut out late night rendezvous with his mates in the local working men's club because the son and daughter-in-law who he lived with worried about him being out after dark. The perceived vulnerabilities and weaknesses of the elderly clearly, I would suggest, form the basis of another controlling stereotype. Given these arguments and my earlier description of the critical contrasting of the young and old by the elderly, it can be argued that in certain respects the elderly operate a total inversion and subversion of the reality of the relationship between old and young as characterized by younger generations, i.e. the old are characterized as strong and the young as weak. Two sources of strength not dealt with in the poem, i.e. (a) strength resulting from historical circumstances, and (b) the transcendence of an essential self over mind and body which is realized in states of mental or physical decline, are, as I have stated, of primary pertinence in this context. I shall turn to these here.

(a) An important part of the perpetual practice of historical critical contrast is the generation of a set of idealized values, ideals, and qualities (for example, communal sociability, cooperation, spend-thriftiness, and domestic managerial skills) which are seen to characterize 'this generation' of elderly people. These are seen as stemming from the conditions faced in their past lives (i.e. poverty, hardship, and the danger and drudgery of work). These too are idealized in this process of historical critical contrast, and are given poignancy by reference to specific historical events which played a significant role in shaping consciousnesses of 'this generation'. Such values and qualities are repeatedly pointed to as exemplification of why these elderly people are well prepared to cope with the rigours of ageing. I have argued that the clubs represent arenas in which the idealized community of the elderly can, through specific practices, through representing a context in which reminiscences may legitimately be enjoyed as one of the main forms of discourse, and through the staging of nostalgic local popular culture, be symbolically reconstituted. In this sense events in the clubs serve to make people conscious of possessing these/their essential qualities which facilitate 'good ageing'. This is one sense in which it can be argued that, at least temporarily, the clubs foster a symbolic mastery over the rigours of ageing.

(b) One of the most striking features of the data I recorded concerns the manner in which people spoke about themselves in relation to their physical or mental decline. One woman stated,

"*Aa get meself up in the mornin' and Aa think to meself, 'wey Hilda another day with this bloody body of yours', It's gettin' that Aa hev to drag meself anywhere noowadays*".

Another woman stated,

"*Aa'm forever forgetting things. Aa'd forget me hoose if it wazn't for the son ferrying us here and there. Aa hev to tell meself what a fool Aa am. 'Are ee reit in the heed hinny', and 'pull yarsell together woman', and the like. It vexes us. Aa get fair worked up ower it so as Aa could hit meself sometimes*".

This curious use of the second person for spelling mind and body cannot be regarded as a linguistic quirk of the area. It is a statement of both, the conscious experience of, and personal distancing from decline.

The sense in which this may be developed into a perceived strength was cogently outlined by a man who referred to himself as, 'Charlie Burnsey, Ellington's unpaid preacher on the meaning of life'. He explained to me that every individual possesses an 'energy' or 'aura' which selects all our thoughts and physical sensations. The individual can learn to contact this 'aura' such that he/she may control these thoughts and sensations. Through telling oneself that, 'these feelings are not mine', the thoughts which constitute depression and the sensations of pain may be dissipated. He stated that whilst some afflictions are inevitable, most may at least be controlled to an extent. In his own case he claimed that his right eye had deteriorated because he had neglected it. The problem initially arose when he was young, at a time when he had not had the practice of contacting his 'aura' and controlling his thoughts and sensations.

Whilst I cannot fully do justice to Charlie's philosophy, a number of pertinent points are raised by this extensively edited account. It reflects points which have been outlined throughout this sub-section; the inevitability of physical decline, but also the responsibility of the individual for the management of the ageing process. In essence, he is suggesting the existence of an essential self which transcends and, to an extent, controls mind and body. When referring to 'practice' he implies that the realization of this self and the consequent realization of its powers come about through the experience of decline and thus, consequentially, the ageing process. This realization reflects the statements of the conscious awareness of decline pointed to earlier. Indeed, Charlie tacitly made the link when in conversations he preached his philosophies to participants in the Ellington day centre.

Other comments people made represent statements of an essential self which transcends mind and body and, thus mental and physical decline. People recounted past events with the use of a range of positive adjectives (energetic, important, sly, and so on), in contradistinction to their current, potentially, negatively perceived selves. Others mixed past and present in conversation without doleful comparison of the state of the person or the value of relative activities in the different time sequences, in between which they had often been badly ravaged by physical or mental decline.

The fact that this perception of a transcendent self as a source of strength in old age cannot merely be considered as just part of the idiosyncratic ramblings of this particular man was evident at two levels. Firstly, many of the participants listened to him attentively and agreed with the arguments he made. Secondly, such agreement was evident in expressed but scantily articulated 'rules' on how to age which reflected his formal exposition. As one woman stated, "*The key is not to weaken, tell yarsell your alreet....keep on tellin yarsell....that's wat keeps you gaan.*"

Other such comments, which often draw upon such perceived bases of strength, refer to responses to the ageing process which are seen as indicative of 'good ageing'. I have identified a number of central features of good ageing. Prominent amongst these are, firstly, stoicism, described variously as, for example, 'keeping a smiling face' or 'keeping your good spirits up', secondly, pragmatic self-sufficiency, i.e. the ability to adapt to the debilitating consequences of illness and to persevere with various activities, or, as it was described by one man, *'the cloot to keep on gaan'*, and thirdly and fourthly, reflecting what I have commented on so far, the ability to put mind over matter and control or psychologically overcome the potential negative consequences of decline through self strength, and display 'corrida'.

Whilst ageing well might not imply a denial of death, the inability to show such responses is seen as tantamount to inviting death. One woman said that she had not visited her daughter in Nottingham at Christmas because she had been ill and feared that she might die away from home (6). Her friend in the club told her that if she didn't get on living without worrying about such things she'd be dead in no time; "*it's the worrying that kills ya.*" People regarded as 'bad agers', i.e. those whose responses are contrary to those outlined, are the subjects of often vehement criticism. For example, one woman who persistently complained about how ill she felt was constantly the source of covert denigration. Whilst some such criticisms were legitimate (for example, she was accused of constantly depressing the other members), others neglected the fact that she clearly was suffering (for example, she was accused of exaggerating her condition in order to attract attention and sympathy which was never forthcoming), and others were clearly fanciful (for example, one woman told me that, "*ney doubt she'll be hoarding good medicines she has ney use for....stoppin' some other poor soul from treatment and doin' the tax payer doon*"). The facts of the covert rather than direct presentation of criticism and its often vehement content, implies, I would suggest, its function as a sanction on those who may feel the inclination to complain.

Conversely, through displaying some of these positive responses individuals gain respect amongst peers. Reward for the display of such responses is an institutionalized part of club activities. At the beginning of club meetings the leaders welcome back members who have been ill (the act of coming back implies the display of some or all of these desired responses) and recount stories of members who have displayed such qualities, and these people are duly rewarded with applause. In addition to this, members who have shown such qualities to a particularly high degree are given gifts. These, I would suggest, constitute prizes.

The encouragement, and desire, of members to participate in the execution of tasks and the production and performance of entertainment must also be seen in this light. Professional entertainment of superior quality is subjected to more intense critical scrutiny than the elderly concert parties. Officials (sometimes described as 'interfering do-gooders') and select bodies of members who interfered or prevented the general membership from actively participating in the running of the clubs were the subjects of vehement criticism. The presence of the professional outsiders and the interference and encroachment of monopolizing helpers, both from within and without, represents a deprivation of access to the activities, upon which personal value depends, and through which the qualities of good ageing can be displayed. The threat is the denigration of the participants, and their being ground down to the status of institutionalized and essentially dying.

A number of related points can be made. First, playing an active part in club affairs does not include caring for other members. Criticism was also directed at members who attempted to take care of ailing members. On occasions one of the members at the Ellington Day Centre would become semi-conscious, drool on herself, and lean against the people she sat with. On the first such occasion one of the women, Barbara, who was sitting next to her tried to clean her face and rouse her from her semi-conscious state. The other women told her to leave her alone. When she began to drowse again, a number of these women assisted her to the back of the hall where they lay her down on a bench, and placed a coat over her to keep her warm. After a while, she began to drool again and started to moan. Barbara got up to see to her, but one of the women firmly took her by the arm and told her to sit down. An argument ensued between Barbara and some of the other women; Barbara insisted that the woman needed attention, and another woman told her that, "*wi divvent come here t' play nee Florence Nightingale.*" This stands in sharp contrast to the events in the old people's home in which Hockey carried out her fieldwork. She found that women cared for and, effectively, adopted weaker women in the institution as though they were daughters (personal communication). The question of institutionalization is central to the difference between the two contexts. It is significant that the example I refer to took place in the day centre, where the members are all 'problem clients' according to the social services; closer than others to institutionalization. The critical reaction of the women was not engendered, as in the case of interfering, by a desire to prevent the denigration of the ailing woman. The women in my fieldwork case were emphasizing boundaries between non-institutionalized and institutionalized. They could not risk their own association with someone who so obviously could not care for herself properly, and, as such, was at risk of institutionalization, when they were, or were officially described as, close to such a categorization themselves. The woman was, in effect, excluded: she became a non-person at the back of the hall and, indeed after a number of weeks was, on the insistence of the club leader, removed by the Social Services.

An interesting issue concerns the problems the clubs had in attracting new members. The act of joining-up is often seen as being tantamount to self-identification as old aged, with all the negative connotations which such an identity involves. Organizers were aware of people's reluctance to join such clubs and in response attempted to foster an image and reality of active participation. However, where their attempts were too zealous it had the same effect of frightening people off. For example, the Buffaloes club insisted that each of its members make an often embarrassing spectacle of themselves by publicly singing a song, occasionally to the accompaniment of an electric organ.

Returning to the main thrust of my discussion concerning the display of the correct responses to ageing, it should be pointed out that whilst, through their adoption of active roles in the club context the participants act as mutual exemplars of the qualities of good ageing, those who are perceived to represent prime exemplification of the correct responses to the ageing process are elevated to an almost totemic status. They act as models of 'good ageing'. It is in this sense that participants prefer the entertainment provided by the concert parties. Quality is of secondary importance. The significance lies in the possession of the revered qualities of 'ageing well'. It is of little surprise that the star turn of the Ellington concert party is not the former opera singer who had succeeded in keeping her voice, but a wheelchair bound blind man who plays the accordion. This point is further exemplified by an incident where a woman in her nineties from one of the concert parties lost her way whilst singing solo. The audience rallied round to join in and accompany her to the end of the song, at which point she was cheered and rapturously applauded. The totemic value of the concert parties is often implicit in their names which draw on metaphors of life; 'The Evergreens', 'Springtime Quartet', etc.

Some people attain an almost legendary and mythological status. Emma Burns, Stan Cowton, and Charlie Burnsey are names I will find it impossible to forget given the frequency with which they appeared in discussion about ageing. Emma was praised for the stoicism she displayed in the face of tragic bad luck. After having brought up between five and ten children with a husband at sea and countless bit jobs to make ends meet she suffered two crippling strokes, but still managed to keep a smile on her face. Her qualities were personified in her nickname: 'The Smiler'. Stan kept on going in the face of adversity. After varying numbers of heart attacks and the constant threat of more he would, as one man put it, "*raise the rafters off while ee was poppin' the heart pills*", and "*when ee's singing them high notes you'd think ees heart was ganna borst*" (7). Charlie was cited as exemplification of the ability to control the problems of ageing through strength. His presence as the oldest member of the Ellington day centre, and his appearance of good health stood as the conclusive evidence of the efficacy of his ideas. Admiration for him was also cultivated by his highly charismatic personality.

Stan's heart attacks and Emma's children). I became aware of this-through talking to Emma who found the stories told about her somewhat incredible and laughable. Charlie was complicit in this process; exaggerating his age and indulging in the creation of a charismatic mystique, by, for example, emphasising his vegetarianism (something quite unusual in these parts), and his knowledge of Greek philosophy, and by claiming that he had been called upon by doctors who believed that he had special spiritual powers which would have a beneficial effect in the operating theatre. Others who became aware of this practice and resented his popularity suggested that he had ulterior motives. He was accused of being a 'ladies man' and at one stage a completely ridiculous and unfounded rumour about him having an affair with a woman some fifty years younger than himself was passed around the Ellington day centre (though I thought it would have been a good idea if he hadn't denied it). In the case of Stan the myth persisted in the absence of its referent, since, despite his much heralded fighting qualities of perseverance, he failed to turn up on all but three occasions in the year that I attended the club. When he did come he implied that his awareness of his value in the club had become oppressive. He felt under pressure to sing when he knew that this would be too dangerous.

Participants' comments suggested that the construction, celebration, and reemphasis of the tenets of the approaches to ageing and physical and mental decline in the social networks of the elderly held a degree of efficacy (i.e. promoting, at least temporarily, a symbolic mastery). People told me that they lived for the clubs. One woman claimed that she could, *"be in bad fettle aall week until club night came around"*, and another woman said that the one night she didn't attend was her, *"sickly night"*. The social construction, celebration, and reemphasis outlined, in conjunction with the entertainment provided by the concert parties provides a potent mixture and stimulates, on occasions, an almost euphoric atmosphere (for example, spontaneous singing, etc.) of liveliness and hope; in essence the feeling of the possibility, and renewed determination to keep on going and age well.

FOOTNOTES

(1) In my proposed paper an the issue of death I will talk about sexual activity as being symbolically indicative of life, and, thus, the assertion of sexual potency and interest as a form of death denial or distancing.

(2) The future paper I will devote to the analysis of pastimes will consider their significance in relation to the question of retirement.

(3) One of the reasons for an inability to give an account here is that I had problems of access to such circles, mainly because of their informality and my gender.

(4) A detailed consideration of the significance of humour in relation to crises faced by the elderly, and particularly in relation to the question of death will be developed at a later stage for publication.

(5) I am not implying that such liberation is somehow an automatic consequence of ageing, but rather that it is perceived to be normal, such that sexuality in old age is considered deviant.

(6) The desirability of death in the community is an integral part of what I have described as the notion of 'good death'. The various facets of this notion will be outlined in a future paper on death.

(7) The implication that ageing well is worth risking life for is implicit in the idea of a 'good death' which will be outlined in the above.

CONCLUDING COMMENTS

The history of Ashington since its inception as an urban area has been one of perpetual turbulence and change. The epoch lived through by the present day elderly is no exception. These changes have had a profound effect on experiences of ageing. Seemingly beneficial changes (increased longevity, greater financial security, etc.) have been accompanied by the continuity or exacerbation of negative aspects of the ageing process. Culturally constructed transitions of ageing emphasize the lowering of status and increased control. The elderly are metaphorically infantalised. Their sexuality is controlled. Controlling stereotypes such as that of passivity persist, even though the potential for antagonism is intensified by ageing itself and social differences between the elderly which have increased as they have become a more heterogeneous social category. Their relationships, particularly to other age groups, are marked by control. The rights to remain independent and to choose the degree to which they organize their lives are undermined by families, care agencies and other members of the elderly in positions of power. Change has intensified the threat of marginality of the elderly in relation to their families, their social networks and the wider community.

The experiences of ageing in the changing social context of Ashington are clearly demarcated by gender. Changes and the rundown of the mining industry have disrupted the relations of power and interdependence between elderly and younger men. The value of elderly women has been eroded by the growth of the state and its assumption of roles within the community which were previously the domain of these women. I have emphasized, however, that whilst men's power and prestige is abruptly interrupted by retirement from waged labour, women's value may be maintained by the continuation of their central domestic and family role.

The situation of male social networks in arenas, such as the allotments and clubs, which are geographically concentrated means that the ability of men to maintain male social contact is often greatly threatened by problems of mobility in old age. In recent years this problem has been exacerbated as elderly men have been forced into using an ever smaller rump of 'old style' clubs. I have argued that, because of women's organizational skills, their contact with agencies responsible for providing leisure for the elderly, the greater numbers of elderly women, and the informality and domestic location of their social networks, this threat is not as great as in the case of men.

However, whilst men face the threat of marginalization and isolation, women bear the major brunt of negative stereotypes of the elderly. Demeaning images of women from throughout the life cycle are given an added power in old age such that women face the double bind of sexism and ageism. This makes the pleasure of participation in their social networks double edged. As I have noted, in old age the absence of men in social gatherings represents conditions under which women feel and experience internalized negative stereotypes to a greater degree.

Moreover, in the representation of negative transitions of the ageing process the elderly woman is the central cultural referent. Her image as sexual yet grotesque renders sexual relations of the elderly an absurdity, and explains declining male sexual potency. The threat of men's potential isolation and loss of power is represented as a movement to a sphere of female control.

In certain respects the elderly are compliant in their denigration (for example, the tolerance of humiliation borne of the elderly Buffs member's need for the charity of the young) and control (for example, their complicity in perpetuating ridiculing and, ultimately, controlling images of their sexual identity). Nevertheless, the elderly are not always passive recipients of control or denigration. I have also shown how they reassert self value by reference to their career roles and new 'retirement occupations' (gardening, caring for younger family members). Other actions represent resistance to control and denigration by others; the subtlety of the woman's provocative dance which challenged the image of ridiculed sexuality; the Ellington Club leader's devious use of the perceived weakness of ageing as a weapon to dispose of interfering young helpers; the co-operation of club members, who aided her in achieving this end, in a carefully planned act of aggressive kindness and statement of independence.

Positive response is also what characterizes the outlook on physiological ageing fostered in the clubs for the elderly. However, rather than denying ageing, as demeaning images are often denied, resisted and subverted, the acceptance of physical and mental decline as inevitable, their confrontation through ridicule and humour, and the management and mastery of the ageing process, through adopting the right outlook, are promoted. These constitute what is termed 'ageing well'.

Totemic figures of good ageing act as exemplars to others. However, the ability to age well is seen to be within the reach of almost all. The elderly are seen to possess specific strengths which stem from their marginalization and this very decline, and, importantly, are seen to be specific to their generation. This is where life histories are most important. They are a resource. They are seen to have left them prepared for the rigours of ageing.

The experiences of ageing, life histories and the celebrated and idealized notion of community are inextricably intertwined. Communal sociability is seen to be a compensation for these hardships. Moreover, these hardships are seen, partially, to have been engendered by the exploitation and regional political favouritism of a world beyond the community's boundaries; hence a scepticism for state agencies of care which effectively leaves it to the individual to manage ageing, despite a celebrated belief of the community to care for its members. I have argued that this celebrated notion of community is characterized by communal sociability and its autonomy and political opposition to agencies such as the state, which are referred to metaphorically in terms of geographical referents, i.e. the south. Despite the importance of geographical referents, such as the south and other local communities, mining is, above all, central to the representation of community. Symbolism surrounding coal and the pit informs the notions of gender and sexual divisions. The hardships which inform the representation of community as characterized by communal sociability, autonomy and political opposition are seen as peculiar to the mining life. Pit work informs language and accent, and coal is the substance by which the area is identified. However, the consequent image of the area and its people as black and dirty is redressed by the symbolic reinterpretation of coal as clean and pure. I have argued that this notion of community is not an accurate reflection of the modern day social milieu. Indeed, the perceived breakdown of its key features is a central concern of the elderly. And, most importantly, it has been deprived of its central referent through the run down of the mining industry. Indeed, a mythologizing of the past suggests that it never existed in the pure and idealized form by which it is represented. However, it is not meant to form part of an accurate social commentary. It represents a set of values of which the elderly are the guardians. It is 'their' community. It is reconstituted in the social arenas of the elderly, and serves a purpose in these contexts. For example, it serves as a basis for a bond of association which transcends social differences between participants in these gatherings.

Within the local context the area of Woodbridge (little more than a large new council estate housing) is as central geographical referent which symbolizes the breakdown of these key features of the celebrated notion of community and, thus also a series of values cherished by the elderly. However, the elderly do not passively stand back and allow this perceived social and moral decline. A dramatic incident in which I played a part is illustrative of this point.

On the morning of the funeral of George Martin (the leader of the Buffs lodge) myself and the men from the lodge met at the club. We toasted him for the last time before his departure, and then left to go to his house where his family were supposed to be having the funeral breakfast around the coffin. We waited at the front door for the coffin to be taken out. One of the men who had gone inside to notify the family that we had arrived returned to tell the others, in some anger, that the coffin was in the kitchen and the family were drinking tea in the front room; "*the' couldn't even bother the'sells t' shift the bloody video set t' mek room for him.*" Moreover, they had left the lid on the coffin because they were afraid it might frighten the children. Worse was to come. We were informed by George's daughter that they would remove the coffin by the back. As the house only had a path at the front there was nowhere for the hearse to park. The younger members of the dead man's family had contravened a series of funerary practices held dear by the elderly men. Most importantly, their insistence that the coffin be removed by the back door showed little appreciation of symbolic boundaries of the colliery home. The men decided to act in the face of what they interpreted as the considerable disrespect of the dead man's family. Regardless of the grief of the relatives, they quite literally hijacked the proceedings. One man who had driven over, parked his car in front of the back entrance to the house, preventing the removal of the coffin. When the hearse eventually took on board its cargo the same man overtook it in an attempt to prevent the driver from trying to make up lost time by taking George on a speedy and disrespectful journey from his home to the church. The event symbolized how cherished notions held by the elderly are under threat, but that even in the death of 'their generation' such change may be resisted and the values of the elderly reasserted.

GLOSSARY

The list of local words here is far from comprehensive. With a few exceptions I have attempted to list those words appearing in the text which are completely different to official English, rather than those which are different by virtue of accent.

Article (The):	Pig.
Aad:	Old (see also Owld).
Bairn:	Child.
Besom:	Fat Woman
Bowk:	Belch.
Bowly:	Coal Shed.
Bubble:	Cry
Bullets:	Sweets.
Buff:	The bare skin.
Byuk:	Book.
Canny:	1-."An embodiment of all that is kindly, good, and gentle....all that is good and love able in a person is covered by the expression, .'Eh what a canny body!.'." (Graham, 1980: 11).
	2-Average, i.e. She.'s feeling canny She.'s feeling not too bad, but not too good either.

	3-Moderate, i.e. Gan canny on the pop. Don.'t drink so much.
Chowked:	Annoyed or fed up. Choked.
Claes:	Clothes.
Clarts:	Wet dirt that is not coal, i.e. mud.
Cop:	Police raid.
Corrida:	Humour or the ability to make humour out of ones predicament.
Cowp:	Turn over.
Cowp hor creels:	Turn a somersault.
Crack:	Conversation.
Dad:	Beat up.
Dar:	Dare. (Darsn.'t. Don.'t dare/didn.'t dare to).
Datal:	Odd Job.
Datal Worker:	Low grade salaried staff in colliery.
Discourse Oil:	Beer.
Divvent:	Don.'t.
Doon-bye or in-bye:	1-Down there. 2-At the pit face.
Dowp:	Backside.
Draa:	Remove.
Ee:	You.
Duff:	Coal dust.

Fettle:	1-Condition, i.e. what.'s your fettle? How are you? 2-Fix, i.e. the windows broken, it needs fettlin.'.
Forbye:	Besides.
Fyul:	Fool.
Gimmor:	1-Sheep. 2-Woman of low repute.
Gissy:	Pig.
Gliff:	A sudden fright.
Grunter:	Pig.
Haddaway:	An exclamation with different uses, for example, .'go away.', .'I don.'t believe you.', .'you don.'t know what you.'re talking about.'.
Hyem:	Home.
Knaa:	Know.
Kyebbling Day:	The day the lots are drawn for the Cavel.
Leit:	Light.
Lowse:	1-Louse. 2-The boss. 3-The end of a working day.
Lugs:	Ears.
Marra:	Male friend (used only by men).
Muck:	Dirt that is not coal.
Nettie:	Outside toilet.

Neit:	Night.
Nout/Nowt:	Nothing.
Owld:	Old (see also Aad).
Pea Soup:	A sludge of water and coal dust.
Plissure:	Pleasure.
Plodge:	Wade.
Poke:	Pack or bag.
Putter:	The worker responsible for moving the coal from the coal face to the conveyors.
Raa:	Row.
Rammy.'s Hoose:	Rammy.'s Ranch was the name given to a scrap-yard in Newbiggin. To describe something as like Rammy.'s Ranch or Hoose is to describe it as chaotic, disordered, untidy, etc.
Reit:	Right.
Sark:	Shirt.
Seam:	Stratum of coal.
Shul:	Shovel.
Sic:	Such.
Styens:	Stones.
Syem:	Same.
Tang:	Smell.
Tap:	Scrounge.

Tek/Tyek:	Take.
Ticket:	Qualification or licence.
Trissure:	Treasure.
Twinin.':	Guiding the coal tub on the rails.
Tyble:	Table.
Varnye:	Nearly.
Waz:	Urinate.
We:	Who.
Wees:	Whose.
Wettor:	Water.
Yacker:	Pitman.
Yark:	Thrash.

BIBLIOGRAPHY
BOOKS AND ARTICLES

Abercrombie, N., Warde, A., Soothill, K., Urry, J., Walby, S. (1988) *Contemporary British Society*, Norwich: Polity Press in association with Basil Blackwell.

Agar, N. (1980) *The Professional Stranger: An Introduction to Ethnography*, New York: Academic Press.

Bloch, M., and Parry, J. (eds.) (1982) *Death and the Regeneration of Life*, Cambridge, Cambridge University Press.

Bulmer, M. (1975) 'Sociological Models of the Mining Community', *Sociological Review*, 23(1).

Caplan, P. (1988) 'Engendering Knowledge: the Politics of Ethnography (Part 1).' *Anthropology Today* 4(5).

Charlesworth, S. (1993) *A Phenomonology of Working Class Experience*, Cambridge: Cambridge University Press.

Cohen, A.P. (1985) *The Symbolic Construction of Community*, London: Tavistock Publications.

Cohen, S. (1972) *Folk Devils and Moral Panics; The Creation of Mods and Rockers*, Oxford: Martin Robertson. (1980 edn.).

Cole, T. (1989) 'In the Dock: Was the Working Class Ever United?' *The New Statesman and Society*, 2(51).

Cowgill, D.O. and Holmes, L.D. (1978) 'Ageing and Modernization', in Carver,V. and Liddiard, P. (eds.), *An*

Ageing Population, Kent: Hodder and Stoughton.

Crouch, D. and Ward, C. (1988) *The Allotment: Its Landscape and Culture*, London: Faber.

Davidoff, L. (1974) 'Mastered for Life: Servant and Wife', *Journal of Social History*, 7(4).

Dawson, A. (1990) *Ageing and Change in Pit Villages of North East England*, unpublished PhD thesis, University of Essex.

Dawson, A. (1998) 'The Dislocation of Identity: Contestations of Home Community in Northern England', in Rapport, N. And Dawson, A. (eds) *Migrants of Identity: Perceptions of Home in a World of Movement*, Oxford: Berg.

Dawson, A. (2000) 'The Poetics of Self-Depreciation: Images of Womanhood amongst Elderly Women in an Englich Former Coal Mining Town', *Anthropological Journal of European Cultures*, 9(1).

Dawson, A. (2002) 'The Mining Community and the Ageing Body: Towards a Phenomonology of Community?', in Amit, V. (ed) *Realizing Community: Concepts, Social Relationships and Sentiments*, London and New York: Routledge.

De Beauvoir, S. (1970) *Old Age*, (transl. Deutsch, A., Weidenfeld., and Nicholson). Middlesex: Penguin Books. (1986 edn.)

Degnan, C. (forthcoming) *Years in the Making: Ageing Selves and Everyday Life in the North of England*, Manchester: Manchester University Press.

Dennis, N., Henriques, F., and Slaughter, C. (1955)

Coal is Our Life: An Analysis of a Yorkshire Mining Community, London: Tavistock. (1979 edn.)

Douglas, M. (1966) *Purity and Danger: An Analysis of the Concepts of Pollution and Taboo*, London: Routledge and Kegan Paul. (1979 edn.)

Frankenburg, R. (1976) 'In the Production of Their Lives, Men (?)....Sex and Gender in British Community Studies', in Leonard Barker, D. and Allen, A. (eds.) *Sexual Divisions and Society: Process and Change*, London: Tavistock.'

Goffman, I. (1961) *Asylums*, Suffolk: Penguin. (1967 edn.).

Gordon, A. (1954) *The Economic and Social Development of Ashington: A Study of a Coal Mining Community*, Newcastle-upon-Tyne: Newcastle University.

Graham, F. (ed.) (1980) *The New Geordie Dictionary*, Newcastle-upon-Tyne: Frank Graham.

Hammersley, M. and Atkinson, P. (1983) *Ethnography: Principles and Practice*, London: Tavistock.

Harris, F. (1980) *Strange Land: The Countryside, Myth and Reality*, London: Sidgwick and Jackson.

Harrison, J (1983) 'Women and Ageing: Experience and Implications', *Ageing and Society*, 3(2).

Hazan, H. (1980) *The Limbo People*, London: Routledge and Kegan Paul.

Hess and Mariner (1975) 'The Sociology of Crime Cartoons', *International Journal of Crimonology and Penology*, 3(3).

Hockey, J., and James, A. (1988) 'Growing Up and Growing Old: Metaphors of Ageing in Contemporary Britain', paper presented to the ASA conference The Social Construction of Youth, Maturation and Ageing. Unpublished.

Kirkup, M. And Thompson, J.W. (1993) *The Biggest Mining Village in the World: a Social History of Ashington*, Newcastle: Sandhill Press Ltd.

James, A. (1989) 'Reflections on an Approach to Understanding Children's Significant Differences', paper presented to the ASA conference 'Anthropology and Autobiography'. Unpublished.

Jerrome, D. (1988) 'Age Relations in an English Church', paper presented to ASA conference The Social Construction of Youth, Maturation and Ageing. Unpublished.

Kerr, C. and Seigal, A. (1954) 'The Inter-Industry Propensity to Strike: An International Comparison', in Kornhauser, A. (ed.), *Industrial Conflict*, New York: McGraw Hill.

Knowles, K.G.J.C. (1960) "Strike-Proneness" and it's Determinants', in Galenson, W. and Lipset, S.M. (eds.), *Labor and Trade Unionism*, New York, Wiley.

Leach; E. (1972) 'Anthropological Aspects of Language: Animal Categories and Verbal Abuse', in Maranda, P. (ed.), *Mythology*, London: Penguin.

Lee, D. and Newby, H. (1983) *The Problem of Sociology*, London: Hutchinson. (1986 edn.)

McCullough-Thew, L. (1985) *The Pit Village and the Store*, London: Pluto Press with the Co-operative Union.

Masterman, C.F.G. (1911) *The Condition of England*, London: Methuen.

Mauss, M. (1954) *The Gift: Forms and Functions of Exchange in Archaic Societies*, (transl. Cunnison, I). Norfolk: Routledge and Kegan Paul. (1980 edn.)

Myerhoff, B.G. (1978) 'A Symbol Perfected in Death: Continuity and Ritual in the Life and Death of an Elderly Jew', in Myerhoff, B.G. and Simic, A. (eds.), *Life's Career Aging: Cultural Variations on Growing Old*, Beverly Hills: Sage.

Newton, K. (1969) *The Sociology of British Communism*, London: Allen Lane.

Okely, J. (1983) *The Traveller-Gypsies*, Cambridge: Cambridge University Press.

Okely, J. (1987) 'Fieldwork up the M1: Policy and Political Aspects', in Jackson, A. (ed.), *Anthropology at Home* - (ASA Monographs;25), London: Tavistock.

Okely, J. (1987) 'Clubs for the Troisieme Age: Communitas or Conflict'. Paper for the ASA conference 'The Social Construction of Youth, Maturation and Ageing'. Unpublished.

Okely, J. (1989) 'Anthropology and Autobiography: Introductory Remarks', Paper presented to the ASA conference 'Anthropology and Autobiography'. Unpublished.

Payne, Bro. M.W. (1952) *The Origin and Development of*

'The Royal Antediluvian Order of The Buffaloes', Leeds: John Blackburn.

Phillipson, C. (1982) *Capitalism and the Construction of Old Age*, Hong Kong: Macmillain Press.

Postal, S. (1978) 'Body Image and Identity: A Comparison of Kwakiutl and Hopi.', in Polhemus, T., *Social Aspects of the Human Body*, Middlesex: Penguin.

Radcliffe-Brown, A.R. (1952) *Structure and Function in Primitive Society*, London: Cohen and West (1963 edn.)

Reed, F. (1975) *The Sense On't*, Newcastle-upon-Tyne: Northern House.

Reed, F. (1977) *Cumen and Gannin: New Poems in the Northumbrian Dialect*, Newcastle-upon-Tyne: Tyneside Free Press Workshop.

Rosser, C. and Harris, C.C. (1965) *The Family and Social Change*, London: Routledge and Kegan Paul.

Sontag, S. (1979) *Illness as Metaphor*, London: Allen Lane.

Szurek, J. (1985) *I'll Have a Collier for My Sweetheart: Women and Gender in a British Coal Mining Town*, Unpublished Ph.D., Brown University.

Tambiah, S.J. (1973) 'Classification of Animals in Thailand', in Douglas, M. (ed.), *Rules and Meanings: The Anthropology of Everyday Knowledge*, Suffolk: Penguin Books. (1977 edn.)

Thienhaus, O.J., Conter, E.A., Bruce Bosnian, H., 'Sexuality and Ageing', *Ageing and Society*, 6(1), 39-54.

Tolson, A. (1977) *The Limits of Masculinity*, London:

Tavistock. (1982 edn.)

Townsend, P (1965) *Aged in the Welfare State*, London: G. Bell.

Tunstall, J. (1966) *Old and Alone*, London: Routledge.

Turner, V.V. (1969) *The Ritual Process: Structure and Anti-Structre*, London: Lowe and Brydon.

Turner, V.V. (1974) *Dramas. Fields, and Metaphors: Symbolic Action in Hunan Society*, New York: Cornell U.P. (1987 edn.)

Whitehead, A. (1976) 'Sexual Antagonism in Herefordshire', in Leonard Barker, D. and Allen, S. (eds.), *Dependence and Exploitation in Work and Marriage*, Kent: Longman.

Williamson, B. (1982) *Class, Culture and Community: A Biographical Study of Social Change in Mining*, London: Routledge and Kegan Paul.

NEWSPAPERS

Ashington Advertiser (Ashington Public Library).
Ashington Collieries Magazine (Ashington Public Library).
The Weekly Courier (Ashington Public Library).

BOOKLETS AND PAMPHLETS

Beamish: The North of England Open Air Museum (1988) *The World of Beamish*, Britain. Beamish Museum.
Channel Four Television (1989) (Dalton, A.) *Dangerous Lives*, London: Channel Four Television.
Coombs, W.B. 'Jack the Coalman and Other Poems'. Unpublished.
Economic and Social Research Council (1984) *The Preparation and Supervision of Research Theses in the Social Sciences*, Luton: White Crescent Press.
Northumberland Health Authority, Social Services and Community Health Council (1986) (Hepple, S.) *Guide Around: Services for Older People in Northumberland*, Newcastle-upon-Tyne: Tyneside Free Press Workshop.
Wansbeck District Council (1986) (McGuiness P.) *An Outline History of Woodhorn*, Newcastle-upon-Tyne: S & P Beals.